Moving On from
Church Folly Lane

D0047389

Moving On from Church Folly Lane

The Pastoral to Program Shift

- ✦ Principles that govern congregational success
- ✦ The maintenance mode tragedy
- ✦ A mission-covenant statement process model
- ✦ A Committee On Ministry model

Rev. Robert T. Latham

Moving On from Church Folly Lane: The Pastoral to Program Shift

Published by Wheatmark®
610 East Delano Street, Suite 104
Tucson, Arizona 85705 U.S.A.
www.wheatmark.com

International Standard Book Number: 1-58736-598-7
Library of Congress Control Number: 2006921378

Contents

Who Should Read This Book

Laity or Ministers?

A colleague of mine shared a different version of the familiar tale of the elephant and the blind men, as told by a professor during his seminary days. This version looks at ministry from the viewpoint of where one happens to be in a church sanctuary. The notion is that things look different, depending on whether one is in the rear, on the side, in the front, or on the rostrum. The metaphorical perception is that despite these differences of perspective, no viewpoint is wrong. They are just views of the same thing from a different angle. Indeed, all together, they make up the whole.

Just so, while it would be true to say that the approach to the congregation's ministry of laypeople and professional ministers is quite different, it would also be true to say that what either does from their particular angle of perspective is no less a significant fulfillment of this ministry. And it would be equally accurate to say that the most profound forms of ministry occur when both are working their different perspective angles with harmonious and mutually empowering intent. Indeed, where both minister and laity exist, nothing of consequence ever really happens in congregational life without their dual ownership of ministry.

The intention of this book is to draw a picture of the different characteristics and institutional dynamics of congregations as they move from one attendance size to another. How such transitions affect lay leadership and ministerial leadership is of a whole. Thus, although distinctions of role will be underscored, there is no intention to address either the laity or professional as separate categories of leadership.

In brief, the reader, whether layperson or minister, is encouraged to read the book and interpret its meanings from one's chosen "viewpoint in the sanctuary." The reader is encouraged to see the necessity of the lay and professional leader working harmoniously from the same page of understanding in order to bring effectiveness out of any transition. Thus, this book is for everyone interested in being part of a dynamic and transforming ministry.

What If My Congregation Is Neither Pastoral nor Program?

Because the Pastoral Congregation (the second-largest attendance size) tends to drag Family Congregation (the smallest attendance size) dynamics into its ministry, the Family Congregation is given some consideration in respect to its basic cultural dynamics and issues. These would add useful perspective to members of the Family Congregation. Moreover, some Family Congregations will be on the verge of becoming or are already in a transition toward a Pastoral Congregation, and this book will give definitive outline to the goals of making such a cultural change.

The largest attendance-size congregation addressed in this book that defines a distinctive congregational culture is the Resource Congregation (often called "corporate"). While it has its own unique characteristics it is also a super Program

Congregation (the third-largest attendance size). Thus, there would be profit in looking at the outlined characteristics of the Program Congregation as found in this book. In addition, the book includes a brief discussion of some of the Resource Congregation's most distinctive cultural characteristics.

On the other hand, a conclusion can be drawn, after considering the assertions of this book, that the number of Resource Congregations in the Unitarian Universalist religious movement are noticeably minimal. This lack of numbers does not discount their importance or contribution. It only assumes that most congregations with potential for effecting social transformation will find themselves within the Pastoral and Program Congregation categories.

*Moving On from
Church Folly Lane*

Introduction

On the Island of Bermuda, at the crest of a hill overlooking the small town of St. George, stand the ruins of an imposing stone structure. Its architectural style is Gothic Revival with arched windows and columns of buttressed pillars. Typical of Anglicanism of the period, its shape is cruciform.

The original purpose of this structure was to replace the older church building down on St. George's main street that had been severely damaged by fire. The congregation began its construction in 1874. However, in 1884, its primary source of financing was diverted to another project, and it had to slow down this construction. As time passed, the congregation became divided about its vision, and in 1894, on the verge of completing construction, it decided, instead, to refurbish and use its old building.

Because of the long history of setbacks and postponements and the final abandonment of the nearly finished structure, one of the streets abutting the property began to be called Church Folly Lane by the local townspeople. Eventually, this name became its officially posted designation.

A metaphor about religious groups that dwell on Church Folly Lane lurks in this story. It is that of congregations that begin projects symbolizing visionary growth but fail in completion and fall victim to maintenance-oriented lifestyles. This is a metaphor that aptly fits the circumstance of many Unitarian Universalist congregations that have struggled for years to complete the transition from a Pastoral Congregation to a Program Congregation without ever finalizing the shift.

However, unlike the St. George church, the reason that keeps most of these congregations in a stalled posture is neither financial nor that of a divided sense of purpose; rather, it is a lack of knowledge about why they are stalled. Even so, deficits that stem from what isn't known can create the same state of folly as deficits that stem from abandoned dreams. The challenge of this deficit may involve any or all of the following:

- perceiving that the shift needs to be made
- understanding the essential differences between the Pastoral and Program Congregations
- accepting what is required to make the shift
- determining a game plan for initiating or completing the shift

Critical to confronting the issues of the shift is becoming aware of the distinctions between these two types of institutions. Many of our congregations have been Program Congregations in terms of attendance for years without ever having perceived the need to consider the manner by which their members relate, the style of basic leadership they need, the nature of their manifested community, the structure of their reflecting organization, or the focus of their decision-making process in contrast with those characteristic of the Pastoral Congregation.

One consequence is that such congregations may continue to organize for failure and tend to call professional leadership that is inappropriate to their needs. The vital resources they expend in ministry simply disappear down a black hole of ineffectiveness. Another consequence is arriving at an attendance or membership plateau that seems impossible to surmount. The cause, in both cases, is likely a lack of awareness of the dynamics that are driving congregational life. Only when this awareness is awakened will the resources expended doing ministry find a maximum and satisfying effectiveness.

Thus, one of the more pressing needs in Unitarian Universalism is to grasp and institute this pastoral-to-program shift in congregational life. On a continental basis, it is possible that up to 35% of our congregations are either trying to initiate or complete this shift. And another very large percentage are already solidly participating in the numerical probabilities of one or the other of these attendance-size cultures without doing so in an effective fashion. These two groups of congregations represent the greatest social and financial influence in our religious movement. Until this shift need is engaged and understanding of cultural differences is grasped, a large number of our congregations will continue to languish in ineffectiveness, and their power to transform will remain at low ebb.

1

Purpose and Resources

Purpose

The specific intention of the following observations is to provide a digested orientation toward the basic differences that exist between the Pastoral Congregation and the Program Congregation and to address some of the critical factors of concern in making the shift between these two congregational modes of existence. The general intention is to show the big picture of why the two types of congregations have such diverse needs. These observations should not be construed as exhaustive. Fuller comprehension of the details of the differences can be gained by reading some of the consulting references listed at the end of this book.

These specific and general intentions are designed to empower the understanding of both clergy and laity so that they can assist each other in making the decisions and commitments necessary to effect the shift and increase mission and ministry effectiveness.

Resources

Church consultants are people who spend their time and mental resources seeking to understand the peculiar dynamics of congregational life and the principles that govern the existence of this type of social institution. Being a small group of people, they tend to read one another's research conclusions and opinions. Out of this pool of collected wisdom, common conclusions arise. Yet, while there might be a general acceptance of these conclusions, there might also be fuzzy edges around them and even disagreements about specifics.

Even though scientific instruments may be used to arrive at reliable data, the conclusions drawn from the data, more often than not, require perceptive creativity. After all, that being studied is the very elusive subject of human group dynamics. In brief, church consultants must place a lot of faith in that form of insight called psychology, and psychology is grounded in preconceived frameworks of reality. Moreover, almost all church consultants, liberal or otherwise, bring, as a part of this reality framework, the perspective of Christianity. On the other hand, whatever their theological persuasion, people will behave as people. The conclusion is that church consultants provide us with valuable insights into the peculiarities of congregational life that empower us to see differently, and thus to behave differently. And they do so despite their theological differences.

The following insights into the shift from a Pastoral Congregation to a Program Congregation draw from the conclusions of church consultants. They also draw from my experiences as a settled and interim minister working with all four of the different types of attendance-size congregations mentioned in this book and the insights other ministers often share collegially from their own experiences. And they are designed to specifically relate to our peculiar Unitarian Universalist religious orientation and the issues inherent in that orientation. Thus, they may shade some church consultants' general agreements in slightly different ways in accommodation to these peculiarities.

One example is that church consultants do not all agree as to the numerical boundaries between these two types of congregations. I have used those figures that accord with my perceptions of the dynamics of our own liberal tradition.

Another example is the special emphasis that I have placed on the role of religious mission as a bonding and directing force in our ministry. Again, this accords with my experience of our congregations having a much lower appreciation for the role of religious mission in the dynamics of congregational life than the typical Christian congregation.

Yet another example is the focal role the Sunday morning worship and educational experience plays in the Program Congregation's ministry apart from the program focus, itself. That is, the Sunday worship and educational experience (children, youth, adults) for the Program Congregation may be, in my judgment, the critical dynamic upon which all others rely for their existence and sustenance.

These judgments also relate to the lack of a common external authority, a common set of beliefs, and a common succinct story, which are motivational resources in Christian congregations. That is, there are dynamics of congregational culture that add significant power to the ministry of Christian institutions that are missing in our religious movement. And almost all church consultants derive their perceptive understandings from the congregational life of some expression of Christianity. However, the burden of motivation tends to fall on other areas of congregational life in our religion's ministry.

Why Consider the Model?

With all of that said and all of these distinctions acknowledged, I suggest five reasons why it might be profitable for a Unitarian Universalist congregation to consider using the model outlined in this book as a guide for enlightenment and a tool for transforming ministry.

1. We generally lack a sense of religious mission and the resource commitment that such brings to institutional life. That is, we lack the two most powerful forces in religion that inform the possibilities of congregational success. Consequently, we remain a relatively unknown and impotent social entity that has a minimal future in the business of human and cultural transformation. This book's model assumes the capacity for both a serious commitment to religious mission and a strong resource base for processing that mission.

2. We tend to rely on technological rather than motivational approaches to membership growth. That is, we seek to induce membership growth through innovative technique as opposed to transformative message or compelling program. Consequently, we are in constant search of new technologies that might enhance our growth through the momentary success of novelty. This book's model assumes a long-term and deliberately designed ministry based on attendance size, by which people will enter the life of the congregation and thus add to its growth naturally and regularly, rather than artificially and sporadically.

3. We lack any comprehensive systems understanding by which to discern the reasons for institutional success and failure or as to why institutional stagnation issues persist. That is, we have no institutional dynamics overview that is capable of eliciting "ahas" about the needs and goals

of institutional living (I reject corporate values as a valid overview for the religious institution). Consequently, we share no common body of perceived institutional principles that govern congregational existence and provide insight about the state of institutional life or the direction of institutional destiny. This book's model assumes a systems set of principles and perceptive understandings that, at the least, informs its conclusions and recommendations with a sense of logic based on broad institutional experience and perception.

4. We persist in relying on static membership statistics, instead of active attendance, as a measure of congregational dynamics. That is, we fail to distinguish between that which might be living and that which might be dying, and the reason for either case. Consequently, we continue to fall for notions that traffic on a one-size-fits-all approach in assessing both programming and ministerial leadership needs and, at the least, stretch too broadly the numerical kinship of our congregations. This book's model assumes that institutional dynamics and needs are best measured by activity, rather than by inertness, and that varied attendance sizes require different means, approaches, and styles of leadership for institutional success.

5. We continue to subtly foster the illusion that liberal religious institutions are different from conservative religious institutions, along with giving credence to the misperception that the more fundamentally conservative the institution is than ours is, the greater is the difference. That is, we behave as if the dynamics that govern dif-

ferent religious social institutions are different because of theological content and unswerving commitment to it. Consequently, we continue to reject those methodologies that undergird institutional social power, because they are used by conservative religious institutions, and we, erroneously, use this rejection as an artificial factor in the creation of a distinctive identity. This book's model assumes that irrespective of the nature of theology and commitment, all religious institutions share the same religious mission and the same methodologies of social power and that true identity differences lie outside this mission and these methodologies.

Aside from the foregoing, the use of this model in my own ministry has been an exceedingly successful tool in awakening congregations as to both their reasons for stasis and for assessing their institutional history and needs. In brief, I have found that it gives a congregation both a clear road map for change and an inspired permission to move into a new future. To say this another way, if a congregation wishes to revitalize its existence, it needs a blueprint for determining where it has been, where it is, and where it can go. It is such a blueprint that provides the ahas of changed perception and the motivations for acting on the ahas. If for no other reason than providing such a blueprint, this schematic is worthy of consideration.

With all of that said, it should still be kept in mind that this is a schematic for understanding and motivation and is not the "gospel" of institutional dynamics. Schematics change as perceptions change. And while some schematics may alter very little over the years and their basics remain applicable to institutional life, they are still subject to change by virtue of advance in human perception.

2

A Perception Is Born

"A transition in size is not just a matter of increasing membership or starting a new and different worship service, but of changing the culture of the congregation."
—*Theodore W. Johnson*

In the Alban Institute book, *Size Transitions in Congregations,* Theodore W. Johnson, Episcopal priest and church consultant, traces part of the history of those most recent perceptions about congregational attendance size that have begun to significantly alter our understanding of religious institutional life. Following is a thumbnail sketch of this history.

Prior to these recent developments, the general perception was that all congregations were the same, only differing in size. The implication of this perception is that all a congregation of any size needs to do in order to grow is duplicate successful programs, organizational structures, and leadership styles that have been developed in other congregations. However, the minimal success rate of such attempts at duplication tends to belie this implication.

In 1983, Arlin J. Rothauge appears to have discovered both why this implication was inadequate and why congregations were not simply size expressions of sameness. Rothauge was a national staff member in the area of congregational development for the Episcopal Church. He was doing research into how congregations attracted and assimilated new members. He published a small book on his findings entitled: *Sizing Up a Congregation for New Member Ministry.* In this book, he concluded that attraction and assimilation depended on attendance size. The attendance size he referred to was the combined total of children, youth, and adults at the Sunday morning worship and educational experience. He identified four basic sizes and made claim that each had a peculiar culture that determined access to membership:

Family (up to 50 attendees)

Membership is accessed by birth, marriage, or adoption. The key leader is a matriarch or patriarch who makes or concurs on all primary decisions. The minister, if one exists, serves as a chaplain responsible for pastoral care and worship.

Pastoral (51 to 150 attendees)

Membership is accessed by relationship with the minister. The minister is the center around which the life of the congregation revolves.

Program (151 to 350 attendees)

Membership is accessed via its programs. The congregation's power lies in the multiplicity and quality of its programming. Ministry is processed through a partnership between laity, staff, and the ministers.

Corporate (351 and up attendees)

Membership is accessed through a variety of ministries whose quality reflects resource capacities similar to those of a corporation. The senior minister is the chief executive officer with mythic dimensions.

Implicit in this schematic was the notion that each numerical attendance size represented a different type of congregational culture that involved how leadership was structured and how relationships were processed.

Many church consultants saw this perception as a potential major advance in understanding the nature of congregational life and immediately began exploring its validity and ramifications.

It is important at this point to again emphasize that church consultants are not in total agreement about the numerical boundaries that separate between these attendance types. Using the best wisdom at my command and factoring in perceptions about Unitarian Universalist congregation dynamics, following is what I perceive to be a useful chart that delineates the lower and upper limits related to attendance dynamics:

- Family Congregation (up to 50; transition zone of up to 75)
- Pastoral Congregation (51 to 150; transition zone of up to 175)
- Program Congregation (151 to 700; transition zone of up to 725)
- Corporate Congregation (701 to ?)
- Mega Congregation (This congregation is well beyond the Corporate Congregation and church consultants have yet to adequately factor in this congregational phenomenon in respect to what attendance begins its peculiar culture. However, at this moment in history, it is not a phenomenon that Unitarian Universalists need be concerned about other than the dynamics of its attraction to the masses.)

The Perception Expanded

Theodore W. Johnson, friend and student of Rothauge, expanded Rothauge's original perceptions in his doctoral thesis. He came up with what he referred to as a companion theory that he called congruence in congregational size. He says: "This theory holds that the principle variables that determine a congregation's type must be congruent with one another for that congregation to function effectively in its type." In this theory he expands on the implications of Rothauge's attendance size postulate and underscores their importance as aspects of the basic culture that defines each type. This expansion and underscoring focus on:

+ *Relationship Style:* how the members relate to each other.
+ *Leadership Structure:* who the leaders are and how they function.

Johnson stresses the importance of seeing attendance size, relational style, and leadership structure as a nexus of those variables that define the peculiar culture of each congregational type. The composite of these variables establishes a characteristic way of being, a sense of self-definition, and a quality of attraction. He places heavy emphasis on the notion that irrespective of the attendance type, all of these variables must be congruent in expression if ministry is to be effective. The degree of effectiveness is commensurate with this synergistic sync.

The Sociological Dimension

What was less clear about these expanded perceptions was how a congregation made the transition from one type to another.

In Johnson's search for such perception tools, combined with resource suggestions from Rothauge, he has presented what he believes to be some clarity about this issue. It is drawn from anthropological research and the claim is that the different types of congregations are created from natural community building blocks. In brief, these blocks are:

Small group (between 12 and 15 people)

What anthropologists call sympathy groups because people who would genuinely grieve over their death generally falls within this numerical range. The small group offers the greatest opportunity for profound relating and is characterized by some form of homogeneity.

Primary group (larger than the small group and up to 50 people)

This group is metaphoric of an intergenerational family where rights and privileges are determined by normal family criteria such as position, gender, age, etc. This may be several such groups or a group formed around a common aspiration. Whatever the reason for coalescing, functioning like a family is its primary characteristic and community is its bonding.

Community group (larger than the primary group but no larger than 150 people)

This group is supposedly the largest sized group in which humans can have active relationships of meaning. The size tends to correspond to typical village size in many cultures around the world. It is characterized by varied communities that need relationship management and is normally governed by a council or some other form of strong leadership.

In this schematic, the Family Congregation corresponds to the primary group, and the Pastoral Congregation corresponds to the community group in respect to institutional dynamics. It seems equally apparent that the Program and Corporate Congregations are created from a variety of small, primary, and community groups.

This is why Johnson suggests that the essential means of transitioning between any of the size type congregations is more than an incremental increase in membership. It is the addition of one or more of these community groups. This is why Johnson calls these various forms of groups building blocks and why he believes they constitute the means by which the transition between congregational sizes can be accomplished with deliberateness. As he states this thesis: "A congregation accomplishes transitional growth by adding new building blocks—small groups, family groups, and fellowship (community) groups—alongside the existing ones, which also may grow incrementally (up to their maximum size) at the same time."

This insight suggests that membership increase without the formation of inclusive and distinctive groupings simply adds to the congregation's roll without adding to its structural or synergistic strength. It is the inclusion through community bonding that unites in a way that captivates commitment. This can be said from a different angle. In the growth of all size congregations, when the limit of their attendance-size effectiveness is reached, new groups should be created. Otherwise, the basic group can continue to grow in membership size without a corresponding growth in participating attendance or an increase in institutional power.

This is also why it is imperative that the construction of any of these groups must include a sense of their commitment to the overarching religious mission of the congregation. Otherwise, they are simply a grouping of building blocks without any bonding adhesive holding them together. They become a conglomerate of independent communities that are housed in the same institution, but this institutional housing is all that they share in common. Thus, their own enhancement and survival becomes the primary motivation in all of their commitments. This fragile alliance of multiple community self-interest groups, then, becomes the character of the larger institution. The end result for a congregation that becomes such an alliance of fragility is a languishing in respect to its own strength and survival. The adding of more building blocks does nothing to empower the fulfillment of its reason for being.

So, it is possible to be successful in adding more independent community groups to the congregation's structural existence without being successful in fulfilling its religious mission. This means that it is possible to make the numerical transition from a Pastoral Congregation to a Program Congregation through the addition of these building blocks without changing the culture or increasing the power of the congregation to be an agent of religious transformation. For Unitarian Universalists, this is one of the most critical transitional pitfalls: to be successful numerically without being successful in respect to either religious mission fulfillment or increased institutional power.

Emphasizing the Nature of Community

While community, itself, is not a unique peculiarity of the culture of any of the four attendance-size types of congregations in Rothauge's schematic, I perceive the nature of the community and how it is manifested to be a distinctive cultural expression of each type for the liberal congregation apart from how members relate to one another. For example, the nature of the Pastoral Congregation is that of a singular bonded community group that manifests itself in an embracing affirmation of mutual worth and a spirit of mutual support that is vital to the success of its culture. So critical to the Pastoral Congregation's spirit of community is this affirmation and support that, when functioning well, it will normally become a prideful part of the congregation's self-identity.

On the other hand, the Program Congregation is a multiplicity of all of the possible community building blocks that Johnson names. If there is a sense of bonded connection between this conglomerate of groups it will only occur if these building blocks share a mutual commitment to a common mission. If this sense of common mission is not present, the spirit of community that members experience will be limited to the nature of the community that exists in whatever groups are engaged through the various programs offered. If this sense of common mission is present, then the spirit of community will be felt, but it will be more diffused in its encompassing nature and of a different quality than that offered by the Pastoral Congregation. This diffusion will announce a different kind of institutional power, and this quality will, of necessity, traffic on nobilities beyond the embracing affirmation of mutual worth and spirit of mutual support of the Pastoral Congregation.

Peculiar distinctions, relative to the nature of the community and how it is manifested, also find expression in the unique cultures of the family and the Corporate Congregations. The nature of the community felt in the Family Congregation will be defined in the same manner of the degree of function or dysfunction characteristic of families and the manner of manifestation will correspond to where one stands in its family structure. The nature of the community in a Corporate Congregation will speak to inclusion in a grand continuously occurring drama and will find manifestation in that broad spirit of connection generated by participating with others in larger than life events. Considering these unique distinctions, it seems useful to add the nature and manifestation of community as one of the variables that constitutes the culture of these different size congregations. Thus, we add: nature of manifested community

Johnson also stresses that when a congregation changes its basic culture, it also has need to change how it is organized in order to process its mission through this different culture. A Pastoral Congregation cannot be effective while being organized in the same manner as a Family Congregation. And a Program Congregation will totally fail to realize its potential if it is organized as a Pastoral Congregation. Attendance size, and the dynamics that issue from such, require a totally different structural focus in the processing of ministry in each of these separate institutional categories. The inability to recognize this necessity is one of the primary reasons why congregations have difficulty in making a successful shift from the Pastoral Congregation to the Program Congregation. The tendency is to continue applying the outdated notion of "one size fits all" to the organizational delivery system when that which is being delivered and the system of delivery are no longer compatible. Because this is of such consequence in making a shift in attendance-size culture, it would also be useful to add the organization dimension to those characteristics that identify the primary distinctions between these institutional categories. Thus we add: structure of reflected organization.

There is another distinctive factor that adds flavor and aids in distinguishing between these different congregational cultures. It is the locus of decision making. While Rothauge and Johnson seem to blend this peculiarity into leadership style distinctions, it seems to me that it warrants a separate category for our congregations.

For example, in the Family Congregation it is the matriarch and patriarch lay leaders who make the critical decisions. In the Pastoral Congregation the minister is the focal point of decision making. In the Program Congregation the locus of decision-making authority comes from a lay-ministerial partnership and is spread throughout the entire organizational structure. The Corporate Congregation relies on its minister for CEO type decision-making guidance. Thus, as attendance increases and congregational cultures change, the locus of decision making moves from lay-led, to minister-led, to a partnership between laity and ministers, and back to ministerial leadership. Therefore, we can legitimately add as another cultural factor: locus of decision making.

This provides us six basic characteristics by which to distinguish between these institutional cultures. While they may shade into each other, they enable us to perceive the nuances of the various attendance types. When all of these dynamics are given due weight, then Johnson's basic conclusion finds additional strengthening: "A transition in size is not just a matter of increasing membership or starting a new and different worship service, but of changing the culture of the congregation." We now have six essential factors in distinguishing between these attendance-size cultures:

+ **size of total attendance**
+ **manner of membership relating**
+ **style of basic leadership**
+ **nature of manifested community**
+ **structure of reflected organization**
+ **locus of decision making**

Church consultants, with many different approaches, continue to do research and apply creative thinking to the dynamics that make up congregational life. The Alban Institute, an interfaith research, training, and publication organization, offers a strong leadership in this area. However, just as there were no final answers in the past in respect to congregational dynamics, there are no final answers in the present. New perceptions continue to bless our understandings. What we must do is to take the gifts of the moment and use them to expand our vision.

3

The Shift

It is important to keep in mind that the crux of this transition is the combined attendance of the adults, youth, and children engaged in the Sunday morning experience. In brief, it is this combined attendance, rather than the size of its membership, that is the gauge of a congregation's vitality. Unitarian Universalists are prone to focus on membership as the hallmark of achievement in congregational life. This is a misperception grounded in corporate mentalities. Vitality lies in activity rather than in numbers. Thus, the baseline for all thinking about this shift in congregational style is viewing it in terms of attendance size rather than membership size.

In Unitarian Universalism, in order to determine need and training approaches, we are prone to divide congregations into small, medium, and large groupings, dependent on membership size. But such ways of categorizing perpetuate the illusion that need is tied to membership size. Such is an illusion because actual attendance in a "medium"-sized congregation may indicate a far more dynamic ministry than the actual attendance of a "large" congregation. Thus, membership as a gauge of grouping congregations into categories of need is both spurious and deceptive.

Depending on the particular consultant, between three and five of these attendance-size shifts are normally identified. The most common views are either three categories of attendance size (small, medium, and large) or four categories of attendance size (family, pastoral, program, and corporate). In our religious movement, when we actually focus on attendance size rather than membership size, we still tend toward the three-category focus because our congregations do not generally grow as large as those of other religious bodies and we see little need to encumber our perceptions with the irrelevant.

However, it seems to me that the four categories of attendance approach is much more definitive in its nuances and we do have a few corporate-size congregations, if the current models of attendance size are used for designation. There is also something to be said for the use of metaphor in making these distinctions, because metaphor speaks to the general character of the congregation being identified. Small, medium and large have no metaphorical meanings. For these reasons, I have chosen to use the four-category approach and the metaphoric pastoral and program labels in my remarks. These labels take on their own significance in the discussion that follows.

For the purposes of this book, the Pastoral Congregation comes into possible being when attendance size reaches around 75 and plateaus when that size reaches around 175. The Program Congregation comes into possible being when attendance size reaches around 176 and plateaus when that size reaches around 725. (See Addendum I at the end of this book for a brief discussion about where the Corporate (resource) Congregation begins and some of its salient characteristics)

Alban Institute consultant Alice Mann has done a lot of research in this area. In her judgment, there is a zone of around 50 in attendance (25 above and 25 below the plateau figure) that comprises a potential "stuckness" area for a congregation evolving through this transition. She calls this the plateau zone. In applying her theory, we see that the Pastoral Congregation may be plateauing in effectiveness somewhere between an attendance size of 150 and 200, and its great danger is getting stuck in this zone. Many Unitarian Universalist congregations will find themselves in this gray numerical area of attendance. This means that a Pastoral Congregation should actually be beginning a conscious shift to a Program Congregation by the time it reaches 175 in attendance size. If it is not, it may be stuck and this stuck place could become its own private black hole.

This notion of possible stuckness underscores another principle of institutional dynamics, namely, that a congregation can end a major phase of its existence without going anyplace else. This is another way of defining the meaning of a plateau in institutional life. In brief, a congregation can achieve the limits of effectiveness of the Pastoral Congregation lifestyle without ever doing anything else except dwelling in the stasis of this ineffectiveness. Another way of saying this is that the fact that a congregation has reached and gone beyond the Pastoral Congregation attendance size does not make it a Program Congregation in respect to its actual function. The reason is that both of these states of institutional being are definitive cultural expressions, as opposed to the simple numerical dynamics inherent in their respective attendance sizes.

Aside from the important dynamics dictated by attendance size, an essential difference between these two kinds of congregations is that one is minister centered and one is program centered, thus the better accuracy of metaphorical labels. It is around these factors of attendance size and centeredness that the other basic characteristics find essential expression and that eventuate in a different community culture.

Before expanding on the implications of these characteristics, six things should be noted:

1. The described characteristics of the pastoral and program postures are not necessarily exclusive to either style. Certain characteristics may be shared by both congregational modes, such as being mission driven or having profound worship experiences. The described characteristics represent tendencies that are pushed by the dynamics of numerical issues and the nature of the institution's center. These tendencies induce struggles that demand shifts in a congregation's cultural perspectives for the sake of effectiveness. In brief, the shift is more complex and less exclusive than the caricature of its described characteristics. Thus, the listing of characteristics is only a conglomerate indicator of those traits that dominate lifestyle.

2. Once a congregation arrives at the numerical threshold that announces the need to address the issues of the shift, the congregation can never be the same despite the desire many will have to turn back the clock. This is the catch-22 of success. If a Pastoral Congregation has a vital ministry and is fulfilling its religious mission, it will grow into a Program Congregation unless there are circumstantial factors inhibiting to its natural growth. So, when a numerical threshold is attained that infuses new dynamics into the life of the institution, the shift is a potential reality that must be engaged, whether positively or negatively. To ignore these new dynamics is to deal with the shift negatively. This is the same as living in a circumstance that demands a new culture for effec-

tiveness while functioning as if the necessity for effectiveness is that of living in an old culture. This posture cancels the potential effectiveness of both cultures.

3. There is nothing inherently better or worse about either the Pastoral Congregation or Program Congregation. Much can be said for the mutual affirmation, support, comfort, and embracing community atmosphere of the Pastoral Congregation in a world increasingly estranged and chaotic. Yet, much can also be said for the excitement, growth energy, and capacity to inspire transformation of the Program Congregation in a world in desperate need of spiritual guidance. Thus, while no one would deny that something significant is lost in the transition between a Pastoral Congregation and a Program Congregation, it must also be admitted that something significant is gained. Any life transition is endowed with simultaneous loss and gain. It is important to acknowledge both. It is this principle of trade-off that must be kept in mind as the issues of the shift are engaged. Otherwise, those enamored of the benefits of the pastoral mode of ministry will only see the loss without seeing the gain, and the will to refocus may also be lost.

4. The descriptions that follow are geared to a generic overview of the shift in question. Congregations will find themselves in a wide variety of different places on the continuum of this shift. Some will be at the beginning of the shift, some will be in the middle of the shift, and some will be toward its conclusion. Others will be in the in-between spaces. Thus, the leaders of congregations who are engaging this material will need to begin where

they perceive their congregations to be in the shift and apply these descriptions accordingly.

5. It is possible that a congregation, for whatever insightful reasons, has already made the shift from a Pastoral Congregation to a Program Congregation and still senses that it is not moving into a new dimension of ministry. That is, the congregation is just on the inside edge of being a Program Congregation. It may still need to engage the cultural principles inherent in its attendance size in order to continue developing its effectiveness. Thus, the congregational leaders contemplating this material may need to ascertain what is not being addressed and make deliberate plans for initiating appropriate movement.

6. It is also possible that a congregation may have been a Program Congregation for years and attained a stasis in its growth. This could be so because it is no longer adequately addressing the cultural principles inherent in its attendance size. Those leaders pondering this material may wish to engender a renewal of perceptions and devotion to the application of these principles that govern its institutional existence.

All six of these observations should be kept in mind as the insights of this book are considered.

4

The Difficulty

The values, perspectives, and rhythms of our culture have obviated the extended family of past history and fostered social alienation. Within this context, a deep desire for community rises from individual spirits that shape human interchange. For decades, one of the primary answers to the question about what people are looking for in their religious experience has been to fulfill this quest for vital community. And the sense of community found in the healthy Pastoral Congregation has made it an appealing place for satisfying this quest.

Yet, the very success of the Pastoral Congregation in bonding people together in specialized community has also been its nemesis. The depth of bonding many feel tends to produce an allegiance that blinds to all other possibilities. The oxymoronic expression of this is the enthusiastic desire to expose more people to the experience of such community life without actually growing in membership. And many congregations live this ambivalence by an inviting/excluding posture that fulfills the need to share the good news while protecting the community from those who would respond positively.

Thus, it is typical of a Pastoral Congregation to arrive at the threshold of its capacity to function effectively and go into a holding pattern that, like a bellows, sucks in members and blows them out in constant patterns that maintain its attendance at a desired level. The means by which this is accomplished is a refusal to alter how things are being done. It is status-quoism. While this may be conscious on the part of a few, by and large, the membership does this unconsciously in instinctive protection of the community and actually wonders why the congregation is not growing.

For such a congregation to move toward becoming an effective Program Congregation, consciousness must be raised on three levels. First there must be exposure to the possible rewards of the Program Congregation mode. Second, there must be an acknowledgement of what will be left behind as it moves from the Pastoral Congregation mode. And, third, there must be exploration of what has to be done to make the transition. With the impetus provided by this new consciousness, there must be a deliberate commitment to making the transition.

While some may welcome this new consciousness and the decision to move forward with the congregation's religious mission, for many it will be a very painful exercise. Indeed, those with the greatest sense of potential loss may become intractably opposed to the shift and exert a lot of energy throwing up roadblocks to the transition. This resistance will be couched in terms of both what is perceived to be in the best interests of the community and that which is sacred and inviolate. It will tend to view any perceptions of need or progress away from the Pastoral Congregation model as enemies of the good.

Enlisting the support of the entire congregation in this transition is an important goal. And all energy expended in this respect will be worthwhile. But as just mentioned, there will be those who cannot see their way to make this transition. Their psychological need for the community support characteristic of the Pastoral

Congregation will blind them to the possibilities of alternative modes of institutional life.

So, there will come a time when the majority of the congregation must assume the attitude that those who resist must either get on board or be left behind. And arriving at this attitude will be very difficult because some members will view the refusal of any members to get on board as a community failure since inclusiveness is such a vital part of the Pastoral Congregation's consciousness. But the congregation that wishes to move on with the transition in terms of fulfilling its religious mission must be willing to put the congregation's best interest above the agenda of individual members. While this may seem a hard decision, retrospect will show it to be the right one.

5

Transition and Change

Consultant William Bridges underscores the importance of distinguishing between transition and change. He suggests that transition is "the inner process through which people come to terms with change, as they let go of the way things used to be and reorient themselves to the way that things are now." This definition sees change as a life imposition and transition as a proactive way of positively dealing with the imposition's demands. But transition and change can also be seen from the opposite end, where a change is viewed as positive and the attitudes needed for transition to this change are defined and deliberately engaged. In this definition change is a goal while transition is the proactive means to achieving the goal.

Congregations that have already arrived at a program attendance size but have not made the cultural shift will need to see change as an existing reality and transition as a proactive way of making a positive accommodation to this reality. In this case, change is the provocateur and transition is the accommodating inner response. Congregations that are on the verge of attendance transition and are exploring the possibilities of making the shift will need to see change as a positive goal and transition as the proactive means of engaging the goal. In this case change is the desired end and transition is the means to the end.

Stuckness Clues

Church consultants also tend to agree about those clues that indicate when a congregation is stuck in this transition, being neither but needing to be the other. Here are a few of these clues:

- The past becomes the frame of reference for success.
- Attendance becomes static and revolving door in nature.
- New members tend to become peripheral in involvement.
- People feel out of touch with the ministry and each other.
- Motivation is low, and blame is high.

These clues also converge to dramatize a maintenance mode in institutional life. A maintenance mode is a form of institutional hibernation that is characterized by a low level of vision, motivation, energy, volunteerism, and financial commitment. Non-growth and drift are its dynamic. Focusing its energies on micromanagement is the primary way it processes its sense of being alive. Energy and resource rationing are its preoccupation, and a few members may be given permission to exert extraordinary control over congregational life because they are willing to invest more energy and resources than most members.

All of this is a reflection of the institution having lost its sense of religious mission. It is the lack of impetus inherent in this loss that permits the congregation to become at ease in this mode. For a longer discussion of what happens when a congregation converts its ministry into a maintenance orientation, see the addendum at the end of the book entitled "The Maintenance Mode Tragedy."

But whatever else these clues may indicate they are also primary symptoms of some form of stuckness.

Stuckness Reasons

There seem to be two primary reasons why congregations grow well beyond Pastoral Congregation function without ever completing the transition to Program Congregation function. These reasons underscore why so much energy is lost to dog paddling in place and why so much discouragement and disillusionment become a normal part of the congregation's way of being.

The first reason is simple enough. There is an unawareness of what this shift is all about amongst the congregation's primary leadership. And beyond this general unawareness there is no framework for understanding the dynamics of the shift. This means there is no vision through which the congregation can attain a different future. There can be no sense of need without consciousness being raised and there can be no successful implementation of this raised consciousness without a blueprint for guidance. Thus, information becomes a key to moving past stuckness.

The second reason is really a perpetuation of the first reason. It has to do with maintaining uninformed leadership. With lay leaders, it is a failure of the congregation to both insist on and make possible the ongoing development of this leadership. Uninformed lay leadership means an uninformed congregation. The insular nature of the typical Unitarian Universalist congregation is a synonym of uninformedness and redounds to the congregation's waste of itself as a spiritual resource. Thus, informed lay leadership becomes a key to moving past stuckness.

The other part of this second reason is that an unaware congregation does not know the kind of minister it needs. It is likely that such a congregation will match its own unawareness in the minister it calls. To do so is to maintain its stuckness. This also underscores the problem of unaware ministerial leadership, which is the broader dimension of congregational stuckness. A congregation will not rise higher than the level of awareness of its primary leadership. Thus, calling informed professional leadership becomes a key to moving past stuckness.

6

Transition and Characteristics

There are congregations who have languished in the transition between a Pastoral Congregation mode and a Program Congregation mode for years without ever affecting the shift. One of the reasons for this is that we cannot control or give direction to that which we cannot name and characterize. Naming is the activity that makes meaning, communication, and deliberate change possible in human experience. To label and give characteristics to the two modes on the ends of the shift in question is to provide both the consciousness raising of identity and the perceptual tool for action that empowers affecting the shift. Thus, the purpose of naming and defining characteristics is to empower both this consciousness raising and effectuation.

Time and Change

The Pastoral and the Program Congregations tend toward opposite views of time and change, two of the major issues of institutional experience. These views are attitudinal and shape the institution's life responses.

In the Pastoral Congregation time tends to be past oriented. The past becomes the frame of reference for what is revered. It is the ground of community identity. Something that has been done for one year may be viewed as having been done always. Thus, change is often viewed as an enemy because it pays no regard to the sacred and alters identity. As a result, the Pastoral Congregation easily endows the status quo with sacredness and easily bows in obedience to the past. To avoid the sacramental pitfalls of this tendency, the Pastoral Congregation must practice engaging change as both sacred and a source of good.

In the Program Congregation time tends to be present oriented. The past will be honored, but it must not be permitted to hold the present captive. Identity involves the past but is more grounded in the "is-ness" of the moment. The present becomes the determiner of the sacred. Thus, the leadership seeks to maintain a view of change as an agent of opportunity and a purveyor of possibility. However, the Program Congregation can slip into a status-quoism of the present by endowing this present with a sense of sacredness that ignores the future. To avoid the rigidifying pitfalls of this tendency it, too, must practice engaging the blessings of change.

In making the transition from a Pastoral Congregation to a Program Congregation, members must willingly unplug from the past and plug into the present. They must come to view change as an ally rather than an enemy. Without making this shift in attitude, the transition will be significantly retarded or simply placed on hold. And, once having made the shift, to prohibit becoming equally stuck in a Program Congregation mode, members must assume the same attitude of openness toward a different future.

Cells and Community

The term "cell" has many meanings. As used here, it refers to a group of people that by virtue of limited size can facilitate the spirit of community belonging in some significant fashion (Johnson's three natural community building blocks). While the Pastoral Congregation tends to be limited in its cellular size, the Program Congregation is multi-celled. The character difference is that it is still possible for the members of a Pastoral Congregation to gather and feel some sense of family connection with most members. However, that experience is no longer possible for the Program Congregation members. And the larger the Sunday attendance of a Program Congregation becomes, the less the possibility for even a sense of extended family to exist. The word "family" for a Pastoral Congregation can be real. For the Program Congregation it can only be metaphorical except in smaller community dimensions. Thus, the problem of facilitating and retaining a sense of profound community becomes one of the critical issues of the transition to a Program Congregation.

There are at least three primary ways of addressing this facilitation of community for the Program Congregation.

Through Purpose

The religious mission of the congregation must be clear and inspiringly stated. It must be elevated as the first priority of every agent of the congregation's ministry. It must invoke commitment to a commonly held "outside our own skin" nobility that transcends personal or small group agenda. It is such a purpose that empowers a profoundness of bonding that survives the fragility of ego need and the competitive spirit of lesser agendas. Without this kind of mission orientation the Program Congregation may fragment into a multiplicity of self-focused and value inflated groups competing for the congregation's attention and resources.

Indeed, the longer the issue of purpose goes unattended, the stronger will grow the sense of independence of these cells from the congregation's mission. They will gradually assume the notion that they exist for the sake of themselves. And, given time to solidify into this state of independence, they may never be willing to reenter the congregation's transcendent mission. When this happens the capacity of the congregation to engage a sense of profound community is significantly diminished, because this profoundness is directly related to its various cells seeing themselves as a synergistic part of a greater whole and grander purpose.

Through Program

The various facets of the Program Congregation's ministry must offer a wide variety of opportunities that enable congregants to establish personal and more intimate relationships of community with other members on a small group basis. It is these kinds of experiences that fill the deep need of people for the spiritual connections that create community. It is also such experiences that validate the transforming possibilities inherent in the congregation's larger religious mission. Examples are covenant groups (small group ministries), spiritual growth classes, spiritual odyssey groups, theology groups, and other opportunities that promote both listening and depth of communication. Adding groups, whatever their size, is a basic program function. In essence, the Program Congregation must offer a continuous stream of bonding activities if it is to maintain the spirit of community.

Through Pastoring

To sustain a sense of community in a Program Congregation, special attention must be given to the program of pastoral care. It is within this ministry that people will feel either embraced or ignored and attribute their feeling to the abundance of, or lack

of, community. Whether it is a baby's birth, a physical crisis, or
a spiritual trauma, if such are recognized in appropriate ways,
the individuals involved feel a sense of being connected to and
cared for by the religious community. To achieve this state of
community normally requires both the devotion of a professional and a vital lay program of pastoral care (pastoral associ-
ates, caring committees, etc.).

The larger the congregation, the greater is the need for
a professional who can give full time to this ministry, along
with giving direction to an organized and trained lay pastoral
care program. The bottom line is that the larger a Program
Congregation grows, the less a single professional minister is
able to care for its pastoral needs, and the greater is the need for
the laity to assume responsibility along with additional professional leadership.

There is a subtlety in the facilitation of community that is
often overlooked in the desire to make efficient use of time in
the Program Congregation. It has to do with the spiritual interaction permitted in meetings by the prescribed agenda. Every
meeting provides an opportunity to do two things that assist
community building aside from the actual work to be done. One
is beginning the meeting with a reminder of the spiritual nature
of the work. This identifies the work being addressed with the
nobility of the congregation's mission and strokes the commitment of those in attendance. This identifying and stroking
places the meeting within its appropriate community context.

The other is the opportunity for members to deepen their
community relationships. A typical way of doing this is to spend
time allowing each person present to share a personal check-in.
There are ambivalent feelings about this activity. While some
members grow weary of it, some members feel it is imperative. The key to retaining the check-in as a way of deepening

connections without allowing it to grow wearisome is to vary its approach. Check-ins do not have to be open-ended in focus such as "this is the state of my psychological being" or "this is what is happening in every aspect of my world." They can be specifically directed in what is requested as a sharing focus, and this specificity can be changed from meeting to meeting. Beyond how this sharing is given focus, it must be carefully disciplined to small increments of time or it consumes the original meeting time purpose and adds to the sense of weariness rather than being energizing of community spirit. If this opening of spiritual interaction is done well with specificity and time discipline, it can become a bonding moment that is anticipated, rather than something dreaded by many of these who will be present.

It should also be kept in mind that using the beginning of meetings as an opportunity to facilitate community bonding need not involve this traditional check-in method. The means of achieving this end can be a creative outlet for its leaders and members. If taken seriously, this creativity can fulfill other participating needs of the engaged members.

It must also be understood that large cells are often just as effective in facilitating the spirit of community as small cells. For the Program Congregation, the issue of community is not only the multiplicity of the cells that are needed, but also the variedness of the size of the cells that are needed. People will be attracted to participate in differing cell sizes depending on the purpose of the cell and the needs of the people. For example, people need larger cell participation so they can feel part of the larger whole. Thus, while small group ministries are vital to certain forms of intimacy they do not fill the total needs for the experience of connected community. As an example, consider larger group meetings such as worship experiences or adult religious education that often involve many people as opposed to a few people. It is not necessarily the size of the cell that dictates the level of the community experienced. The focus and quality of what happens is equally important.

The Program Congregation must deliberately design what it does in order to address effectively the issues of cell division and community. Otherwise, it becomes a consumer-oriented religious corporation dependent on designing program product that elicits the loyalty of satisfied customers. In so doing its mission to transform the world is lost to the singular focus of pleasing the private agenda of its individual members and addressing their momentary whims.

Professional Leadership

The Pastoral Congregation tends to be most concerned with spiritual comfort and family maintenance. Thus, it wishes its professional leadership to be the head of the extended family, relate as friend, and model feet of clay. On the other hand, the greatest need of the Program Congregation is spiritual challenge and institutional effectiveness. Thus, it wishes its professional leadership to provide big picture guidance toward institutional power, relate as mentor, and model provocative insight.

Totally different leadership skills and totally different leadership outlooks on institutional life are needed in these differing types of congregations. The bottom line is that the professional minister of a Pastoral Congregation can survive with low institutional skills as long as relational skills are high. On the other hand, the professional minister of a Program Congregation can survive with low relational skills as long as institutional skills are high. This is why the professional minister who succeeds in the Pastoral Congregation could be a failure in a Program Congregation or vice versa. However, this does not mean that professional ministers cannot move successfully from one to the other. But it does mean that if there is to be success in this move, there must be a corresponding understanding of the shifts in modes of leadership that are required, along with the will and ability to make the necessary accommodations.

Another professional leadership issue in this transition has to do with the size of this team. The Pastoral Congregation tends toward a mom-and-pop store mentality. It does not wish for too many heads of the family. It wants things to be simple and straightforward. It is an institution that does not wish to be an institution. Thus, a single minister or a mom-and-pop type team of ministers maximizes its comfort level. It may also have other staff members but these are viewed as subservient to the direction and need of father, mother, or mom and pop.

Conversely, the Program Congregation tends toward multiple ministers and staff. It does so because it soon learns that its available pool of volunteers usually have neither the time nor the skills to fulfill its enlarged and complicated ministry demands. Moreover, these volunteers are now beyond being motivated by family dynamics. The operative principle is that the larger the congregation grows the greater is the need for more ministers and staff that reflect diverse skills and commitments and who have the time to do the necessary work. In the effective Program Congregation this inevitably translates into a significant number of professional ministers and staff, both full and part time.

This multiplicity of ministers and staff, while solving one problem, also contributes to another. They are too many and too narrowly focused for the congregation to know intimately as in a Pastoral Congregation. Thus, its members must become satisfied with the trade-off of friendship and intimacy for skill and provocativeness. They must be willing to shift their expectations of the institution from comfort to challenge. This is not to say that friendship, intimacy, and comfort will no longer be available. If the issues of program and pastoring are being addressed in appropriate fashion, these needs will be available through a variety of means. But it is to say that the general character of the congregation's experience with professional leadership will be provocation and challenge. Those who wish a more intimate and friendly relationship with professional leadership will only find that possibility in positions of lay leadership that require constant contact with one of these professionals.

A third leadership issue has to do with leadership authority. In the Pastoral Congregation the professional minister spends the bulk of time and energy developing and maintaining a personal relationship with the members, doing pastoral care, and cultivating the spirit of community. This activity makes the professional minister the center of community attention. The very nature of this kind of intimate relating with congregants makes the professional minister the most influential member of the religious community. In this respect, intimacy breeds authority. This accords with one definition of power, which is measured by increments of attention. The Pastoral Congregation minister gets loads of attention and, thus, is greatly empowered. Power is one of the ultimate forms of authority. When there is need for a task to be done, the minister is in a position to draw on the power of this relating to recruit the necessary leadership. This binds the community even tighter around the person and leadership of the professional minister.

On the other hand, in the Program Congregation, there are too many members for the professional ministers to have friendship relationships with, let alone intimacies. The power to influence must be drawn from other sources. Normally, this power will flow from three primary areas. One is the capacity of the professional minister to inspire toward spiritual growth and mission fulfillment, whether this is in a meeting or in the pulpit.

This is the same as establishing the credentials of personal and institutional wisdom.

Another source of empowerment is the ability to recruit and train lay leaders to do what the institution needs to have done. This requires the skill to create training designs that empower others. That is, rather than winding the life of the institution around their own being, they must be able to create circles of power beyond their being that flow outward in linear fashion through the being of inspired and trained lay leadership.

A third empowerment source is the will to minister directly to the needs of the congregation's leadership. While the minister cannot meet the pastoral care needs of all the members, she/he must be attentive to the needs of the laity and staff that form the key leadership team that gives direction to congregational life. This ability to inspire, train, and care for basic leadership needs is the source of much of the Program Congregation minister's institutional power. It is the power that is gifted because of a responsive appreciation for recognized vision, skill, and caring.

There is no substitute for the capacity to inspire for a Program Congregation minister. However, all ministers do not posses the skills to train. In this event, the minister must have the insight to recognize the training needs and create the thirst for the training. Beyond this, there must be a will to enlist those who can do the training. If the minister has identified the training need and inspired its fulfillment, this is equally an attribution of wise leadership.

Here is a summary. Professional ministerial authority in the Pastoral Congregation tends to be attached to the person filling the office, while in the Program Congregation it tends to be attached to the office that the person is filling. Or, in the Pastoral Congregation the institution revolves around the professional minister, while in the Program Congregation the professional minister revolves within the institution.

Lay Leadership

There is also a basic difference in the lay leadership of the Pastoral and Program Congregations. In the Pastoral Congregation the community is small enough, and the institutional needs simple enough, to revolve around a single leadership figure. This single figure is the minister, and lay leadership tends to be self-submissive to the minister's direction. This does not mean that the laity do not lead, rather, that they tend to take their cue for leadership in any new direction from the minister. This cueing is strengthened by the knowledge that they were probably chosen by the minister for their position or at least endorsed for the position by the minister prior to selection.

But in the Program Congregation, the institution is too complex and there are too many positions representing the various facets of ministry and too diverse a skills level needed for all leadership to be provided by the minister and staff. For any real effectiveness, this leadership must be spread out amongst a large number of laity. This spreading does two things. First, it underscores the ownership of the mission and ministry of the congregation by the laity. And if the Program Congregation is to be successful, this sense of ownership must be strongly grasped by the laity.

In the Family Congregation (the predecessor of the Pastoral Congregation), the ownership of the mission and ministry is in the hands of a few lay leaders, to the exclusion of both the rest of the laity and the minister. In the Pastoral Congregation, the ownership of the mission and ministry belongs to the minister by virtue of the central role gifted to her/him by the laity. In the

Program Congregation, the opportunity of the total of the laity taking ownership and sharing this ownership with the minister and staff is an essential phenomenon of making the shift with full effectiveness.

And this introduces the second thing, namely, the potential of shared ministry becoming the focus of all involved. Shared ministry is the practice of that belief that when the laity and the ministerial leadership arrive at mutual visions, respect what each brings to the table, and work in a partnership, all of the energy and resources expended combine in common focus and mutual empowerment. There are two institutional axioms involved in this transaction. One is that the greatest power to create positive change derives from common focus. The other is that power shared is power multiplied. When a congregation lives these two axioms through shared ministry, the synergistic power of this mission and ministry is maximized because members, ministers, and staff are on board with the congregation's reason for being and view it as the property of the whole.

Thus, when a congregation begins making the shift from a Pastoral Congregation to a Program Congregation, if it wishes to plumb the fullest potentials of this shift, careful attention must be given to lay ownership of the mission and ministry and to those attitudes that foster the spirit of shared ministry.

Sunday Worship

Because of its relational focus, the Pastoral Congregation can be engaging despite poor service design and poor preaching, because the family has gathered to celebrate its own being as a beloved community, and the minister is its beloved head. If this sense of community is strongly felt, it may even see its experience of community worship as synonymous with being spiritual. On the other hand, the program church cannot be engaging without exciting service design and stimulating preaching, because the community has gathered to experience provocative insight and spiritual challenge. So, it is the service itself that must provide the basis for whatever sense of bonded community is experienced during worship.

Because of this shift from relational worship to challenging worship, in order to be effective, the Program Congregation must have a dramatic worship experience. This drama involves all elements of the experience from music to preaching. The larger the congregation, the greater is this need, for it becomes the only touchstone for the majority of the members with the congregation's life. This means the worship experience becomes the congregation's primary impetus for maintaining member commitment to its mission and ministry. Thus, the ultimate characteristic of worship leadership must be a natural reflection of mission and ministry commitment presented in an inspiring and challenging manner. Creativity is an added bonus.

In the Program Congregation, the worship service bears another burden, that of the shift in motivating its members' spiritual growth. Because the congregation's attendance and dynamics are beyond extended family appeal, there must be an attraction inherent in the service that excites spiritual provocation and transformation. While sensing the spirit of community is important, it finds that it is no longer sufficient to maintain allegiance. Whatever the form of worship and whatever its style of leadership, it must elicit a sense of drama that captivates the individual worshipper and draws them into confronting their personal life journey within that of the congregational community and the existing world. Otherwise, they will only return on Sunday morning when there is no other more compelling attraction to claim their time commitment (a Starbucks and the *New York Times,* for example).

This ties into the primary focus of the Program Congregation, which is its program. It is the worship experience on Sunday mornings that constantly reminds the membership of the growth possibilities that are inherent in its larger program ministry. The Sunday service provides a hint of what might be in store for those who engage this programmatic ministry. It announces the possibility of pursuing a greater depth.

The bottom line is that the worship experience in the Program Congregation carries both the necessity of holding high the nobility of the religious mission as a bonding source for its disparate parts and of provoking sufficient spiritual growth as to compel sustained commitment and attendance. The strength of its ministry and its continued numerical growth will be closely related to its capacity to fulfill these two necessities.

The worship experience is vital to both the Pastoral and Program Congregation. The distinction is that they tend to celebrate different values and carry different burdens. And this is so even if similar structures might be used.

The Board

Because of the smaller size of the Pastoral Congregation its available volunteers are fewer and its leadership foci are more concentrated. The board of trustees is an example of this concentration. Usually, board members are representatives of the various facets of the congregation's ministry. Thus, when the board meets so does the program council and the finance experts because they are one and the same. With this dual focus, the board micromanages both the business and program life of the congregation simultaneously. Being the primary prestige lay leaders of this strongly bonded community serves as its own motivation for making the time commitment necessary to fulfill this dual focus. Moreover, being on the board provides an opportunity for the laity to relate in more intimate fashion with the minister and the minister is also normally able to influence the filling of this leadership body with quality members with high-level skills.

Church consultants agree that dynamic growing congregations share some similar characteristics. Generally, at the top of the list are a clearly stated mission, mission-oriented leadership, and an organization that reflects the mission.

When a congregation achieves the attendance size of a Program Congregation, there is a corresponding need for a shift in the focus of its board of trustees. The board needs to become the primary lay body of mission-oriented vision and spiritual leadership in congregational life. This means it must shed its traditional role of micromanaging the affairs of the congregation. No board of a Program Congregation attendance size can, with any adequacy, perform both of these roles at the same time.

One of the ways it sheds this traditional role is to delegate the authority for micromanagement to other agents of ministry. A specific example is the creation of a Program Council that assumes much of the board's former role in program development. And still another example is the creation of an Executive Team that can meet often and make rapid and sensitive decisions having to do with the congregation's administration and operations. Yet another is the concentration of financial management in a single team that can keep the entire ministry envisioned and focused.

Until the board of a Program Congregation makes this shift it will not be able to provide the lay leadership necessary for the congregation to take full advantage of the possibilities of its attendance-size status. This is the same as saying that as long as the board is providing Pastoral Congregation leadership (business and program micromanagement) to a Program Congregation (policy and vision macro-management) it will be a retarding factor in the fulfillment of the institution's mission and ministry.

Because of the recognition of these leadership needs in the Program-size Congregation, there has been, in recent years, a growing interest in what has come to be known as policy governance. Primarily, this is an attempt to translate the basic principles of John Carver's model for transforming secular corporate boards into the life of a voluntary religious community.

While this translation is creative, often depending on the attendance size of the congregation, the essentials of the policy governance model tend to remain the same. This involves a small Executive Team doing the micromanagement of church affairs with the board being freed to organize itself as a mission-oriented policy body that gives visionary leadership to the church. This also involves allowing other authorities to flow outward from the board to all its agents of ministry. In brief, shared power and encouraged creativity are two results of moving to a policy governance model.

It may be that it will never be possible for a Program-size Congregation to take full advantage of those opportunities its status offers without going to some form of policy governance that lifts board leadership out of the time and energy consuming role of micromanaging church affairs and converts it into a body of mission and policy leadership. Certainly this is true of simple effectiveness.

A major requirement of making this alteration in leadership style is trust. The board must trust its Executive Team. The Executive Team must trust all the agents of the congregation's ministry. The congregation must trust the board and the Executive Team. But the issue of trust in leadership is a key to any successful transition from a Pastoral Congregation to a Program Congregation, irrespective of the model of board leadership employed.

In a Pastoral-size Congregation, the processes of consensus and democracy tend to not only be cherished but to be highly guarded in respect to infringement. They are often made synonymous with and endowed with sacred qualities. When a congregation achieves the status of a Program Congregation, its very size militates against the possibilities of large-group consensus and effectiveness requires that the privileges of direct democracy be reserved for those critical decisions necessitating general membership support and that a greater investment be made in representative democracy.

This is not an easy shift in mentality to make when one has basked in that fullness of decision making afforded by the size smallness of the Pastoral Congregation. But it is necessary, otherwise the institution's decision-making processes become captive of the holding patterns of time. And its energies, rather than being focused on mission and ministry, are absorbed into the complexities of the decision-making drama itself.

Since the necessary movement in decision-making processes is from the whole to the part in the larger Program Congregation, this, again, requires a significant elevation of trust in those leaders who comprise the parts. In a religious movement whose people normally only trust their own personal judgment, this shift of releasing one's judgment to others requires a decision of deliberateness.

This is why it is also critical for the Program Congregation's modes of ministry to be driven by policy and that these policies become the focus of congregational concern as opposed to decision micromanagement. And this is why the policy governance model is so appealing. It releases the board of trustees to create policies geared to the congregation's mission and to monitor the application of these policies throughout the institution's life.

When accepted policy is the basis for decision making in all areas of the congregation's ministry, two things become possible. One is that a uniform gauge for judging effectiveness is created. The other is that trust is facilitated because the criteria for decision making are already in place. But, whatever the mode of decision making, the Program Congregation's membership must shift into a leadership trust posture or it will find its energies to fulfill its ministry deflected toward extinguishing the fires lit by paranoia.

The bottom line is that the Program Congregation must exhibit two strong characteristics if it is to be successful. It must have mission-driven leadership and the congregation must trust this leadership. The two feed each other with empowerment.

Organization

As earlier mentioned, another critical factor present in powerful growing congregations is an organization designed to facilitate its mission. This design is essential for it guarantees that the congregation's energy will flow toward mission fulfillment. This, of course, is the intended purpose of organization as announced in the accepted principle that form follows function. However, when institutions make a shift in how function is to be accomplished they do not always perceive the need to make a form accommodation. Such a lack of accommodation inevitably results in low-level effectiveness.

Thus, when a congregation makes a shift in institutional dynamics as a result of attendance size, this shift necessitates looking at its organization to be sure it is not only an efficient user of energy but also allows that energy to flow in directions of mission fulfillment. Often, this is not considered at all in the transition from a Pastoral to a Program Congregation. There are several reasons. One is that the transition is gradual. While this gradualness leaves the membership feeling they are still the same, the dynamics of institutional life have been changing around them. This changing requires different ways of perceiving and doing that must have corresponding organizational reflection if effectiveness is to follow.

Another reason is that sometimes a congregation is aware of the need to revitalize its mission-covenant statement without also being aware that the organization may need the same revitalization. A principle operative here has to do with how to determine a congregation's real mission irrespective of its stated mission. The two are not necessarily the same. The way to make this determination is to totally ignore the announced statements of mission and look at where the congregation gives focus to its greatest amount of energy. That is, do a spiritual energy audit. It is this energy focus that announces the real mission because it is where the congregation is primarily invested. And, as a rule, the organization reflects this real mission. Thus, revitalization incorporates not only the perspective of mission but also an organization that facilitates this perspective.

What all of this means is that it is not possible to have an effective ministry as a Program Congregation by using the organizational structures of a Pastoral Congregation's ministry. While the essential religious mission of the two may remain the same, the means of accomplishing that mission are altered by the dynamics inherent in their respective attendance-size cultures.

Here is an example. Often, the board of trustees of a Pastoral Congregation incorporates the functions of a program council and a finance committee as well as its own traditional functions. This multiple functioning accomplishes several things. It addresses the issue of too many tasks and too few volunteers and it simplifies decision-making processes. It also reflects the congregation's lack of cellular complexity. As a congregation grows in size, cellular structure, and complexity, this simpler way of organizing the board of trustees overloads the decision-making process and fractures its energy focus. In brief, it becomes inefficient, burdensome, and unwieldy. For the Program Congregation it is a way of organizing toward failure and demands a restructuring that facilitates toward success.

Following is one way of visualizing three primary foci that address the organizational needs of the Program Congregation. In whatever way the congregation determines to fill these needs, it becomes a creative endeavor. And what they are called is secondary to providing the focus. It should also be kept in mind that these three foci constitute a big picture framework that facilitates the total of ministry. What distinguishes between them is the nature and limit of focus. The one thing they all have in common is the goal of empowerment.

Focus:	Governance	Administration	Program
Nature:	Policies	Decisions	Growth
	Assessments	Processes	Challenge
	Directions	Communications	Community
	Boundaries	Operations	Outreach
Agent:	Board	Executive	Councils

Until these three areas of ministry focus are designed and functioning synergistically, the Program Congregation will suffer a loss of effectiveness and diminishment of mission fulfillment.

When we apply the term "pastoral" or the term "program" to the term "congregation" it is an attempt to describe a basic identifying characteristic. Pastor is a word that designates a leader whose primary investment is in looking after the well-being of the flock of which she or he is in charge. This characterization means that the life of the congregation is in the pastor's care and its existence is wound around its relationship with this pastor. In essence, the pastor stands at the center of the congregation's existence. And as goes the pastor so goes the congregation.

On the other hand, the term "program" applied to a congregation implies something radically different. The term "program" refers to a predesigned agenda that deliberately gives specific direction to all expressed energy. A program abhors chaos. It wants to maximize the possibilities inherent in the happening. It wants something to be accomplished. It is goal-oriented.

With this in mind, the Program Congregation uses program to fulfill its mission. It creates a slate of programs for this purpose. These programs are designed to facilitate both its internal ministry to members and its external ministry to the world.

Its internal ministry, like a mini-seminary, produces spiritual enlightenment and prods toward spiritual growth, which is the harbinger of personal transformation.

Its external ministry, like a change agent, infuses society with alternative values and invites different realities, which is the harbinger of social transformation.

It is the congregation's program ministry that is the doorway into the life of the congregation and into the life of the community in which it exists. This means that the congregation must be willing to invest both people and monetary resources into making its program ministry a highly visible and powerful reality.

There is no particular type or style of leadership necessary to success in this programming thrust except that which is capable of seeing the big picture and, correspondingly, creating and facilitating powerful and potentially transforming events. This means the Program Congregation is just as dependent on leadership as the Pastoral Congregation. The difference is that this leadership is multiple and cannot happen if the leadership, itself, is the agenda because, oxymoronically, the agenda is independent of the leadership even though it depends upon it.

Thus, the Program Congregation is an institutionalization of multiple agendas processed by multiple leadership, all of which have a unified and specific plan to empower the congregation in the fulfillment of its singular religious mission. And the leadership of the Program Congregation is devoted to keeping the fulfillment of this mission as the focus of all of these agendas and to developing further agendas that might empower an even greater fulfillment. Both the institution and its leadership exist for the sake of this singular mission and the elevated empowerment of its message of personal and social transformation.

To say all of the above differently, the Pastoral Congregation is focused on the leadership of its professional minister while the Program Congregation is focused on the leadership of its professional programs (inclusive of Sunday morning). Both may be into fulfilling their religious mission but the means and focus of accomplishment are radically different.

The Committee On Ministry

The Program Congregation has grown to an attendance size and a multiplicity of cells and programs that require a form of overview leadership for success. This leadership must provide an oversight of mission and ministry that is unencumbered by other responsibilities, biases, or constraints. It needs to provide constant education and inspiration relative to this mission and ministry so that the congregation does not lose sight of its reason for being amidst its swirl of activity. And given the multiplicity of cells and programs competing for resources and vision attention and the multiplicity of leaders processing this competition, there is need for an effective independent agent that can do mission education, ministry effectiveness assessment, and conflict management in a manner that inspires toward ministry fulfillment and safeguards the well-being of the congregation's life and does so in a redemptive manner.

Boards that have not moved away from a micromanagement mode are too busy micromanaging to provide such big picture spiritual leadership. And even if a board has shifted to the more effective mode of leadership of some form of policy governance, its focus will be primarily on the congregation's organization and vision as related to the policies and boundaries established by these policies. In other words, it is very unlikely that a board can provide this kind of overarching leadership and still be effective. It has the governance of policy boundary effectiveness and total institutional vision to care for and that is quite enough for its plate, particularly if it does so with spiritual and mission intention.

One of the primary reasons for the creation of the Committee On Ministry was to provide such an overview body of spiritual leadership that was not biased by attachment to any particular segment or function of the congregation's ministry but had as its only goal the spiritual well-being of the congregation and operated with no authority except the stature behind its own composite being.

Unfortunately, this original design has been tweaked in so many different directions that a large number of presently existing Committee On Ministry models are relatively ineffective. So just having a Committee On Ministry will not necessarily serve this need for an overview leadership body. The Program Congregation that wishes to fulfill its religious mission with maximum effectiveness will want to look at a model of the Committee On Ministry that has proven itself in terms of its original design. Only such a model will fill the need for the big picture leadership that will be essential for its success.

It should be kept in mind that the Committee On Ministry, as conceived here, is not the same as a Ministerial Relations Committee with a new title. A congregation that has an effective Committee On Ministry needs no Ministerial Relations Committee because professional leadership is understood to be only one component of its larger ministry and every component of ministry is viewed as critical to success. Professional leadership is given its rightful weight within the congregation's ministry but it is not seen as requiring a special advocate. It is the whole ministry that is the advocacy of the Committee On Ministry.

The ministers and staff of a congregation that has such an effective Committee On Ministry will be supportive of this body's purpose because they know it will address the needs and issues related to their roles in the congregation's ministry with the same diligence it addresses all other ministry needs. They know that what is in their own best interest is a vital and effective ministry of the whole. Thus, they will give their full support to this body's overarching leadership capacities. The only exceptions will be those whose egos are threatened by the inherent power of such a body.

7

Comparisons

Following is a brief listing of differences between the Pastoral Congregation and the Program Congregation. Again, this listing is a reference to tendency driven by all of those peculiar dynamics of attendance size and borders by nature, on caricature. It is designed to provoke flavor through category rather than expressing definitiveness. A tendency toward does not necessarily mean that the goal of the tendency is either missing or present. It only means that, given all factors, this would be the normal direction of congregational leadership and life. Nor does it mean that the opposite of the tendency is no longer being provided. For example, a Program Congregation's tendency may be toward a spiritual growth orientation but this does not mean it is not providing those foci necessary for the experience of community. It is important to not read tendency as meaning exclusivity.

Issue	Pastoral	Program
Cells	Few	Many
Orientation	Relationships	Programs
Desire	Comfort	Growth
Worship	Community	Challenge

Issue	Pastoral	Program
Time	Past	Present
Change	Threat	Opportunity
Organization	Simple	Complex
Decisions	Broadened	Narrowed
Authorities	Minister	Multiple
Minister/s	Caretaker	Mentor
Minister Skills	Relational	Motivational
	Embracing	*Inspiring*
	Comforting	*Training*
	Supporting	*Crafting*

There are some evidences that one has become enamored of either the Pastoral or Program style of ministry. A single piece of evidence may not be sufficient to draw conclusions but a number of pieces together provide a strong hint.

Pastoral Mentality

- Attachments to "Mom and Pop" views of professional leadership.
- Caution in major decision making without the affirmation of professional leadership.
- Desire to have a sustained personal relationship with professional leadership.
- Tendency to judge all professional leadership by a Pastoral Model.
- Adult programming is wound around professional leadership.

+ Devotion to worship styles that focus on celebration of community and spiritual comfort.
+ A defensiveness as regards anything that might threaten established modes of community.
+ Preference for total community-oriented decision-making processes.
+ Tendency to sanctify toward non-change.
+ Exaggerated sense of congregational identity.

Program Mentality

+ Appreciation for mentoring models of professional leadership.
+ Preference for spiritually challenging and motivationally inspiring worship styles.
+ Interest in a multiplicity of provocative growth-oriented lay-led programming.
+ Desire for organizational structures that focus and maximize the positive effect of energy investments.
+ Comfort with a many-celled institution bound in unity through common purpose.
+ Excited by the possibilities inherent in change.
+ Trust in smaller and multiple decision-making bodies.
+ Appreciation for organizational collaboration.
+ Expanded sense of identity.

It should be kept in mind that making any kind of major institutional shift is rarely, if ever, a single holistic leap. It is normally done gradually with one aspect of the shift helping facilitate another aspect of the shift until finally all major aspects move harmoniously in such a way as to signal that the shift has been completed. That signal is a metaphorical hum that runs through the organizational life of the congregation. It is a hum that emerges from the spirit of synchronicity.

Following is another way of approaching where the congregation might be in reference to this shift. Consider this listing as an aggregate of signs.

Issue	Pastoral	Program
Personal Need	Everybody should know I have a need	I need to let people know I have a need
Decisions	I should be in on most decisions	I must trust others to make the right decisions
Growth	We don't want to get too big	Where will we put the people?
Annual Meeting	Let's dissect everything	Let's not micromanage
Community Goal	Fulfilling my personal hopes	Reaching others with our ministry
Minister/s	Relate to me	Mentor me
Pledging	We must justify the spending	I will give toward this vision
Vision	We need to strengthen our community life	We need to reach beyond ourselves

Issue	Pastoral	Program
Staff	Why isn't the present staff sufficient?	We can't do it without more staff
Attitude	We must include everybody	We must be more effective
Question	Am I being served?	Is the world being served?
Framework	The practical	The potential

It is important to note that a focus on community creates gauges of success and failure that are geared to the needs of those whom the community is seeking to embrace. This internalized form of ministry is natural to the focus because the intent is to enfold all within the whole in a warm and satisfying manner. Thus, while this may appear on the surface to be self-centered it is, in reality, only a symptom of the focus. This same symptom will appear in the smaller cell units of the larger Program Congregation.

As previously indicated, the requirements of professional leadership in these two types of congregations is significantly different. This does not mean that a minister cannot stay with a Pastoral Congregation as it grows into a Program Congregation. Many ministers have a large supply of orientations and skills. What it does mean is that the minister who has enough institutional savvy to leap across this transition and continue to be an effective professional leader will also perceive the need for a major shift in how leadership is exerted.

Following are a composite listing of some of the major components of what will be required of ministerial leadership in both of these types. A minister may not need every facet of character and all the skills listed but will certainly need a sufficient combination to be successful.

Pastoral Congregation Minister

Characteristics
- community orientation
- empathy
- compassion
- rewarded by helping people in a selfless manner
- ego health
- is not impressed with self-authority

Skills
- listening
- relationship management
- pastoral care
- counseling
- teaching
- administration
- self-renewal

Burnout
- trying to meet the needs of pastoral care and friendship of more than 150 active members
- inability to lay aside the individual burdens of the active membership

Program Congregation Minister

Characteristics

- big-picture orientation
- institutional wisdom
- rewarded by partnerships and social transformation
- ego health
- can share authority

Skills

- facilitation
- training
- organizing
- bonding
- crafting
- inspiration
- worship
- power management

Burnout

- trying to minister to everyone rather than focusing on the basic lay and staff leadership
- inability to release control to other leaders

8

Obstacles

There are numerous obstacles to making the shift from a Pastoral Congregation to a Program Congregation. The primary obstacle is overcoming the membership's devotion to the culture of the present in order to move into the culture of the future. Nothing is more difficult for humans than to make a cultural shift.

When traveling to another country of the world we do so for the specific opportunity of momentarily experiencing differences of culture. However, actually moving to that same country on a permanent basis would require major changes that could plug into personal resistances grounded in notions of safety, communication, perceptual nuances, levels of comfort, and preferential attachments to the cultural norms that must be left behind.

The Entire Body

The shift from the Pastoral posture to the Program posture will elicit some of the same kind of cultural resistance because the purpose of the shift is to live in a different culture. The Pastoral Congregation's character of mutual affirmation and mutual support that eventuates in the notion of total concerted community movement is a perfect example. The spirit of this perspective is that of consensus very similar to a political educational euphemism widely used during the first part of the present century: *no child left behind*. Broaden this philosophy to *no person left behind*, and the attitude of many Pastoral Congregation devotees is captured. As it is with the educational version of this philosophy so it is with the religious version of this philosophy. The goal is for the entire body to move in concert. Thus, if there is anyone who is not persuaded to move with the total group, this implies a failure on the part of the group to fully affirm and embrace every member or achieve a consensus in decision making. This gauge of failure tends to become endemic to the general attitude of the Pastoral Congregation's membership.

However, as the Pastoral Congregation grows it becomes more and more difficult to maintain this consensual approach to community life. And as it achieves the limit of effectiveness of its attendance size this attitude simply becomes a bog in which decision making and forward movement become mired. Often, the end result is that the community becomes captive of its own distinguishing feature and may either spend all its energy trying to maintain an upright position in the bog or exhaust all of its energy trying to pull every member through the bog. Thus, while the affirming, embracing consensual approach to community works well for the Pastoral-size Congregation, it actually becomes a millstone when applied to its transition to a Program-size congregation.

The problem that emerges in moving to the Program Congregation culture is that not everyone will wish to make this shift and no amount of embracing, affirming, and consensus seeking will change this resistance. Members that have not been able to divest themselves of this mentality will feel a deep sense of failure in not being able to persuade those who do not wish to be persuaded and will want to expend energy vital to the transition on continuing to seek this persuasion. The inability to move beyond this aspect of the Pastoral Congregation culture will be one of the major obstacles to the transition to the Program Congregation culture.

Others

There are other potential obstacles that might hinder this transition. Here are a few of the more common.

In respect to attitude:

An unclear and uninspiring mission statement

While many congregations have a mission statement, the tendency is for them to be nothing more than a large umbrella statement of facets of ministry rather than a succinct statement of actual mission. Not only are these lists uninspiring, they are confusing as to what is the real mission of the congregation. Moreover, when it becomes necessary to judge the effectiveness of the congregation's ministry, there is no meaningful gauge by which to do so, because what is being used is form rather than function. This is similar to using a product as a gauge by which to judge it rather than using the goal model that inspired its production. It is to use a symptom by which to gauge a symptom.

Without a true statement of mission, it is difficult for a congregation to stay on track with why it exists let alone be inspired toward moving into a different future. And this is to say nothing of the identity issue that is critical to attracting new members. Particularly is this so for Unitarian Universalist congregations who are required to establish their identity without aid of a common dogma.

The other issue that might make mission an obstacle has to do with substitution rather than clarity and inspiration. The Pastoral Congregation is usually so heavily invested in community as an end to itself that it tends to gradually see the provision of this kind of relating as its mission rather than that of offering transforming answers to life's compelling questions of mystery. It may be so enamored of the social community it has created that it becomes very difficult to grasp the notion that community created from mutual transformation is far more profound and far stronger than community that exists as an end to itself. Thus, for those with the heaviest investment in the experience of community as their reason for membership, the very idea of evolving into a Program Congregation may seem a violation of religious purpose.

A mindset that applies solutions of simplicity to issues of complexity

As a congregation grows in attendance so does its complexity of relationships and needs. The attempt to constantly address complexity with simplicity only compounds the issue of complexity. The move from the simpler issues of the Pastoral Congregation to the more complex issues of the Program Congregation requires both opening the doors of creativity and seeking alternative wisdoms.

A failure to relate the attraction of quality to motivation for both joining the congregation and staying motivated within that membership

One of the great dangers of the Pastoral Congregation is to fall prey to the "dirty sock syndrome." If a pair of dirty socks is left on the living room floor and stepped over enough it will become invisible to those who live in that space. Often, the Pastoral Congregation will confuse lack of a quality environment in both facility and worship as a synonym of homeyness. This is much like inviting a guest into the living room and assuming that the host being comfortable with the room not having been cleaned is a compliment of acceptance of the guest as "just family." Guests are more likely to see the dirty sock or lack of cleanliness as evidence of lack of pride and relate that lack of pride to the values being espoused by the host.

This lack of an understanding of the power of quality and a failure to invest in its meaning may be one of the more subtle but powerful unrecognized reasons why Pastoral Congregations get stuck in the transition toward a Program Congregation. Membership does not grow because people are not being drawn into a qualitative message of commitment.

False debates that focus congregational energy away from the real issues

An example of this obstacle is the growth versus non-growth debate over membership size. The attitude of this debate is: "We believe we have an option as to whether our congregations will grow or not grow." A subtle support of this belief comes from denominational leadership that offer congregations growth strategies or growth programs when they "choose" the growth option. Obviously, the belief is pervasive in our religious movement that growth is an option of choice.

But, pervasive or not, is it true? Do we have the option? The answer is only yes if the question is divested of religious purpose. That is, we can only choose between growth and non-growth if our congregations exist for the sake of themselves. However, if our congregations partake of the same mission as all other religious institutions, which is a purpose outside ourselves, then the answer is no.

While this distinction may seem subtle it is, in actuality, critical. It is critical because a congregation that is doing its religious mission cannot help but grow because this very doing will make it dynamically appealing and socially transforming in its ministry.

Moreover, a congregation that is doing its religious mission would never be having a debate over growth versus non-growth because fulfilling its mission is the focus of its energies. Its issues would revolve around how to accommodate all the people who are being attracted to its ministry. It would never occur to it to have a discussion about whether or not it ought to limit this attraction.

The congregation that has concerns about how growth might impact its comfort level needs a different debate. The issue it needs to be debating is: "What is our religious mission?" And once that has been determined the next issue of debate it needs to engage is: "Shall we be driven by our religious mission or some other mission?" Ultimately, the growth versus non-growth debate is a symptom of congregations that have opted not to be religious institutions with religious missions. Thus, the growth versus non-growth question is not only irrelevant for the religiously mission-driven congregation, it is meaningless.

A different version of the growth versus non-growth debate is a nice comfortable social club for liberals versus a congregation that impacts its social environment through its ministry presence. The reason why it is a different version is because those who do not wish to grow are usually those most likely to be comfortable with being nothing more than a liberal social club. A religiously mission-driven congregation, again, would not even think of a comfortable social club for liberals as an option to being large enough to create social impact. Mission orientation is always preoccupied with generating the power that can change the world that surrounds it. It does not view itself as an oasis, which constitutes an invitation to escape from the realities of its surrounding world. Rather, it views itself as a change agent in the world.

The reason why the foregoing debate versions are important to congregations making the Pastoral to Program shift is because making the shift is not only induced by growth, it is sustained by growth. For the congregation devoted to religious mission, this growth will come naturally. The only "growth strategy" this kind of congregation needs is how best to engage its mission in the circumstance of its peculiar cultural existence. Seeking growth for the sake of growth draws attention away from its mission and introduces the artificial as a substitute.

In respect to actualities:

Inadequate facilities for inspiring growth

This may relate to issues such as being overcrowded and being unwilling to either go to two services or building new space or starting a new congregation. Church consultants believe that when a sanctuary is 80% full the message is that there is no more room available for new people. This message is the same as a no vacancy sign.

This may relate to unkempt and rundown facilities. Such is a message about quality that says the congregation has a low level of pride. This message normally rubs off on the congregation's beliefs and the whole is rejected by newcomers.

Outmoded organizational structures

When a Pastoral Congregation is close to making the transition to a Program Congregation there is a corresponding need to reorganize to fit a different perspective about how the religious mission is to be accomplished. Without this reorganization the energies invested through old structures will not produce desired returns and will begin creating the frustration of ineffectiveness. In turn, this frustration will drain the energies needed to start or complete the transition and the institution easily becomes characterized by burnout and low energy.

Lack of adequate staff and equipment

As a congregation grows the responsibilities and demands of the professional ministry increase. So does the need for staff that processes programs and communications and manages the building and grounds care. And as these needs proliferate so does the need for the equipment that technologically helps process and supports ministry needs while decreasing energy output drain.

Often, due to the time span that occurs as a congregation moves toward the necessities of shifting to a Program Congregation mode, both equipment and staff needs go begging until they reach a critical point. Unfortunately, by the time this crisis occurs the congregation is often in those financial binds that seem to preclude the possibility of addressing the crisis. However, even a deliberate but long-term plan is better than wallowing in the slough of despond. Even if other aspects of the ministry need to be placed on temporary hold, the congregation must figure out a way to deal with the need for adequate staff and equipment because they grease the wheels of transition as well as solidifying gains.

Counterproductive expectations about ministerial leadership

This is continuing to anticipate that the minister will respond to congregational needs from a Pastoral mode when the necessity is to respond from a Program mode. Such expectations are twin to the inability to reconcile being organized as a Pastoral Congregation while attendance dictates the necessity of being organized as a Program Congregation. Essentially, it asks for the minister's energies to be directed toward maintaining the past as opposed to moving toward the future. It is to call for a "maintenance" style of professional leadership. It is expectations that assume leadership success while subtly energizing leadership failure.

The Family Congregation Influence

There are no clean-cut shifts made between any of the identifiable congregational cultures pushed by attendance size. People will be in various states of perception and response as the congregation moves in new directions. It is what dominates the congregation's concerns that will be indicative of where it is at any given moment rather than a uniformity of congregational mindset.

Because of this it is useful to know some of the basic characteristics of the smallest of these cultures called the Family Congregation. The reason is that members and leaders who have been around since the congregation's early history may carry some of its original Family Congregation dynamics through the congregation's shift to a Pastoral Congregation and into its shift toward a Program Congregation. And these embodied dynamics can have significant negative effect on the drama of the shift. Moreover, people with a Family Congregation orientation may join both the Pastoral Congregation and the Program Congregation and engage the ministries of these congregations as if Family Congregation mentalities were the only valid reality.

The Family Congregation behaves as a single cell organism. Its attendance size is up to 75, with its plateau zone between 50 and 100. Its descriptive title speaks volumes about its dynamics. Lyle Schaller is one of our culture's preeminent church consultants. In breaking down the size dynamics of a congregation he uses more than four primary categories. His smallest grouping is for up to 35 in attendance. He uses the metaphor of a cat to describe the characteristics of this size congregation. While the four-category model combines Schaller's breakdowns, the characteristics of his smallest size finds ample expression in the Family category.

When speaking of the smallest size congregation he asks this question: "How many of you have ever owned a cat?" But it is a trick question. He is quick to point out that those who think they own a cat do not understand cats. He uses this as a springboard to talk about small congregation characteristics. Here are some of these character observations:

+ You cannot own a cat; you can only keep a cat.
+ A cat will not work for you but you may work for a cat.
+ Cats are independent in spirit and self-sufficient in attitude.
+ Cats take care of themselves and do not like dependence.
+ Cats are basically untrainable. They function off of instincts.
+ Cats have nine lives and can survive poor organization, uninspired atmosphere, shoddy environment, neglect, and abuse.
+ Cats don't seek advice and don't feel they need training.

Other observations about cats may also be pertinent to their behavior:

+ Cats are not into becoming anything other than what they are.
+ Cats determine when they wish to be stroked.
+ Cats will scratch you if you try to control their behavior.

Much of what one might infer from this listing probably traffics in some measure on Family Congregation dynamics, depending on the nature of individual congregations.

Despite the sense of bristly independence implied in Schaller's metaphor, it is easy to become enamored of the Family Congregation because it offers extended family dynamics to its members. This is both its blessing and its bane for, like a typical family, it can be either functional or dysfunctional. And, again, like the family, this functionality tends to self-perpetuate into a lifestyle. Whichever of these possibilities dominates the lifestyle of the Family Congregation will, in all likelihood, root back to its inception. That is, it will be grounded in why it was started, how it was started, and who started it.

On the blessing side, this size congregation may function through a healthy relationship between its members. Thus, there will be levels of satisfaction, joy, and caring in its spirit of community that will encourage its members to behave out of their noble capacities. If this is the case then, unless there are naturally inhibiting environmental factors, the congregation will eventually grow into a Pastoral Congregation size. Its very success will cause it to grow beyond the inherent capacities of a family orientation and enter new dynamics requiring different ways of expressing its mission and ministry. While this transition may not be easy it will be facilitated by its very character of healthy relating.

On the bane side, this size congregation may function through unhealthy relationships between its members. Thus, there will be levels of discontent, spite, and manipulation in its community spirit that will encourage its members to behave out of their ignoble capacities. Because of this character it will normally either not grow or it will engage a constant pattern of growth and regression that will become the same as non-growth.

If a Family Congregation decides to live its bane possibility, then, moving its relationship style toward health will require deliberateness. And deliberateness recognizes the need for change, the cause of bad health, and designing a means of addressing both in a consequential fashion. However, it is usually difficult for members relating in an unhealthy way to admit a complicity with family dysfunction. Yet, without such admission there is little purchase for deliberateness to occur. Thus, the help of a skilled consultant may be required for the congregation to rise out of dysfunction into function.

The catch-22 is that if the dysfunctional Family Congregation is going to Call or hire such a consultant, its financial resources encourage linking up with a novice. While good fortune might combine this newness and a consultant with previous applicable skills in another career, there is no guarantee of such good fortune. Therefore, district and denominational leadership must design programs that make skilled consultancy possible if they wish this religious franchise to represent a more profound witness to the movement's faith.

There are at least three attitudes that sometimes rise in the Family Congregation that relate to the professional ministry. One is a prideful: "We can do whatever needs to be done and we don't need ministers to help us." Another is a more negative reactive posture to the authority traditionally inherent in the calling and training of professional ministers that translates into an anti-clericalism. It must also be acknowledged that these attitudes towards ministers do not necessarily dominate the Family Congregation's membership and may find expression in other size congregations as well. The levels vary from congregation to congregation and reflect different experiences with ministers as well as certain psychological temperaments. And some Family Congregations may exhibit little of such attitudes along with a high appreciation for professional leadership. The only thing important to remember is that such negative attitudes may be lurking in the background of some member's attitudes when the congregation is discussing the role of professional ministers in the transition from a Family Congregation to a Pastoral Congregation.

A third attitude toward ministers is inherent in the nature of the dynamics of the family-oriented institution. The minister may not be viewed in any negative fashion at all. Indeed, there may be genuine appreciation for what the minister brings to family life. The notion that the minister's function is limited to that of being a chaplain is simply understood as a part of the power structure of the Family Congregation.

This is not necessarily a view that implies a lesser valuation of the minister's role in congregational life. It simply may be accepted as natural to the family's structure of relationships. After all, in this size congregation, ministers come and go in quick succession and often leave with various levels of tension existing between themselves and the congregation over the caution the congregation may display toward proposed new programs, growth strategies, and visions the minister advocates. If these proposed directions are not applicable to the dynamics of the Family Congregation's culture or are pushed with uncommon enthusiasm, this only further raises the caution level of members and often eventuates in a suspicion of anything new that ministers, particularly those with limited experience, might propose. Members soon learn, in this quick turnover of ministerial presence, that the people they have to relate to in the long run are the lay leaders and that it is in their best interest to not allow a rift between themselves and these leaders. In brief, if a choice has to be made about whose leadership they will follow it becomes very apparent as to the wisest choice if family inclusion and comfort are the judging criteria.

Moreover, the fact that ministers do not stay around very long causes members to see them as outsiders, despite the vital role they might play on behalf of the family. Thus, for this size congregation, the minister is rarely viewed as a family member (unless it is someone who has risen through the ranks from lay status). Usually, the best the minister can hope for is adoption. But adoption requires time and the achievement of a certain stature in the family.

In brief, attitudes toward ministers may span a variety of attitudes that range from negative to positive. The savvy minister finds out what these might be and adjusts his or her ministry accordingly for effectiveness. The single factor that usually signals a change in this way of relating to the minister is the growth of the congregation that necessitates that the membership come to rely more and more on the pastoral and friendship role the minister serves with size increase. This is the same as beginning the transition from the Family Congregation to the Pastoral Congregation.

Just as in most extended families, certain roles are accrued by its lay members by virtue of congregational birthright, needs, skills, and actual biological family relationships within the membership. Church consultants give these roles functional labels such as Patriarch, Matriarch, and Gatekeeper. Those who assume these roles are endowed with the power to direct family life. This power may simply be influence or it may constitute tangible control such as over the congregation's finances. Either way, the power is real. The tendency in maintaining this power is to build up both an expertise and control over some facet of the ministry that seems indispensable to the congregation's well-being. This assures sustained empowerment.

Roy W. Oswald, Senior Consultant for the Alban Institute, suggests that the purpose of the minister in the Family Congregation is to serve as Chaplain and the purpose of the Matriarch/Patriarch is to keep the minister from taking the congregation in some new direction of ministry. The tongue-in-cheek nature of this suggestion only emphasizes its ground in reality. This strongly infers that the locus of power in this type of institution is the laity and, specifically, certain laity.

Whoever, within the life of the Family Congregation, represents these roles cannot necessarily be known by looking at a current list of those holding official titles in the congregation's leadership registry. These people may not fill any official role. But those who hold official titles know whom to consult in order to process any major decision that might affect the family's lifestyle. And they know better than to move with such a decision without first gaining the blessing of these hidden leaders. In brief, a few people normally control the life of the Family Congregation and they may or may not be readily visible to anyone new to the congregation.

What all of this means is that the minister of a Family Congregation is in a unique position that is not necessarily on par with professional ministry in other types of congregations (it is well to keep in mind that the role of the minister in all four of the categories of congregational types is different). The minister must lead, circuitously, through those lay leaders who are actually in control of congregational decision making. And, even to lead effectively in this regard, the minister must have a great deal of acuity and earned respect.

If the minister is around long enough and the lay leadership "adopts" her/him into the "family," this empowers above the norm but is still not that empowerment that can stand on its own and buck the family's actual leaders. Thus, if a minister is to be successful in a Family Congregation, he/she must be patient, content with circuitous leadership, and skilled at power locus influencing and understand that small progress is huge progress. This is simply the nature of this style congregation. But despite the peculiar position of the minister in the Family Congregation, her/his leadership is critical to the membership developing a vision of its potential and realizing its growth possibilities.

When the Family Congregation is successful and grows in attendance size and begins shifting into a Pastoral Congregation, two things can happen. One is that the minister's role and influence in congregational life will grow correspondingly. The other is that these unofficial lay leaders can significantly influence whether the shift is facilitated or retarded. Once people experience how power strokes their self-worth it becomes addictive and may translate into a personal lifestyle need.

Even if a congregation makes the shift from a Family Congregation to a Pastoral Congregation, these lay leaders may still exert significant influence over the congregation's destiny. Particularly might this be the case if they have supported the shift and gained further empowerment in the doing.

Many years ago I became the first minister of a Family Congregation trying to make the shift to a Pastoral Congregation. Prior to my arrival upon the scene the traditional roles of the professional minister had been divided between a small group of influential laity. For example, one was administrator, one was counselor, and one was preacher. My arrival and covenant of agreement, ipso facto, officially relieved this group of these facets of professional leadership. I had the good fortune of recognizing what had happened and how their sense of loss was playing out in resistance to my own leadership. So, I sought to empower them in all possible ways. However, their sense of self-worth was so intrinsic to the roles they had been playing that they were unable to view a professional minister's presence as anything but threatening to their personal worth stature.

These were all good people who had a long-term devotion to the congregation's growth and future. When the time came for the congregation to move in new directions, such as calling a full-time professional minister, they gave very positive leadership to this move. Yet, when that move became a reality they saw it as threat rather than blessing and it took years to overcome their negative leadership and for the congregation to grow to an attendance size that, within itself, become disempowering of this group.

Fortunately, for many congregations, this kind of empowered laity is able to detach their self-worth from their congregational roles. They are able to move into a place of more mature power that does not confuse these two dimensions of living. Thus, they are further empowered by the congregation that sees not only strong commitment but also elevated wisdom in their presence. Those who have assumed such roles of special empowerment may become either a force for movement or stasis in a congregation's life. They, themselves, make this determination.

Many congregations have a short enough history that the people who represent this type of lay leadership are still in membership and still exerting influence. Some of these lay leaders have actually been with a congregation as they have shifted from a Family Congregation to a Pastoral Congregation and are involved in the shift to a Program Congregation. Such lay leaders can be very positive forces in helping the congregation complete this shift. They could rightfully take great pride in endowing the congregation with a legacy of lay leadership that brought the best of the past into the present but never allowed the past to become an obstacle to the future.

The more the spiritually healthy Family Congregation grows in attendance size the greater will become the membership's appreciation for and reliance on ministerial leadership. This growing reliance is a major factor in the ability to empower the congregation toward transition. What this means is that even though the Family Congregation may seem to be an immovable object, it is not. Size dynamics encourage perceptions of new needs and accommodating changes. Growth in attendance institutes these dynamics.

In brief, if a Family Congregation is being successful it will grow and will be required to wrestle with transitioning to a Pastoral Congregation culture in the same way that the success of a Pastoral Congregation requires that it wrestle with transitioning to a Program Congregation culture. One of the key signs that the congregation is being successful in this transition to a Pastoral Congregation is the gradual elevation of the role of the professional minister, beyond that of the Matriarch/Patriarch, as critical to the spiritual life of the congregation.

It should also be kept in mind that some small congregations are started by groups of people who have a high level of appreciation for professional leadership and who have as a part of their basic game plan the Call of such leadership at the earliest possible moment. These Family Congregations tend to avoid a lot of the tension and negative drama that accompany the existence of those started with lesser vision.

To round out the image of the Family Congregation both in terms of its difference from the Pastoral Congregation and the possible influence of members who remain enamored of its dynamics while incongruently being in a larger size congregation, reviewing those six facets that comprise its cultural outline may be useful.

Size of Total Attendance

The dynamics are governed by upwards of fifty children, youth, and adults on a Sunday morning.

Manner of Member Relating

The internal relationships are metaphorical of an extended family. The head of this family is a Matriarch or Patriarch, or both. All other members will relate to these heads and each other as defined by age, biological relationship, length of membership, reason for adoption, gender, etc.

Style of Basic Leadership

The Matriarch or Patriarch (or both) provide the congregation's primary leadership. Other lay leaders will provide further congregational leadership under the approval of these key determiners. If a professional minister exists, she/he serves as a chaplain whose primary responsibility is worship and pastoral care. Any significant leadership exerted by the minister outside of these two areas will normally occur circuitously through the Matriarch or Patriarch.

Nature of Manifested Community

The spirit of community will be consistent with that of an extended family. And, like a biological extended family, the spiritual health of this institutional community will range on a continuum between being functional or dysfunctional. Knowing everyone in a manner that fosters the sense of community as kinship is bedrock for the Family Congregation.

Structure of Reflecting Organization

As a small single cell, the Family Congregation is organized with simplicity to facilitate the social dynamic of the extended family.

Locus of Decision Making

All major decisions will be sanctioned by the Matriarch or Patriarch, who always represent the laity and who give essential direction to this small internally focused community.

The Peculiar Deficit

Whatever the institutional issue, modern Unitarian Universalists bring to it a peculiar deficit that has to do with motivation. Nowhere does this become more apparent than during a time that either requires the need of a transition to be confronted or the need for it to be implemented. The reason is that dealing with transitions successfully requires a state of deliberateness and deliberateness is a property of motivation.

Here is the background to this deficit. Most religions have a nexus of factors that serve as a unifying force in community life. Normally, these factors are inclusive of a common source of authority, a common succinct story, and a common belief system. And those religions that seem to be most powerful also tend to have some common musical or tonal touchstone that deepens the emotional content of these bonding factors. This broad spectrum of commonalities is normally infused with a devoted sense of religious mission. Together, these common- alities and this mission devotion make for high motivation that fuels the requirements of social power.

Modern Unitarian Universalists seem deeply threatened by the very notion of commonality. In awkward compensation, we seek more subtle and fragile bonding alliances through avowed common values while, oxymoronically, stressing the virtues of difference, variety and individualism that all tend to militate against any depth of bonding.

Moreover, while there are two long parallel religious narratives that background our historical existence, there is no pithy story that gives us a common center of identity. Nor is there a common external authority or an agreed-upon creed that might unify beyond this lacking story. And while we have a generally acknowledged common hymnal, there are few unifying psalms and no tonalities other than a classical bias. This decided lack of unifying factors diminishes motivation to the fulfillment of personal agenda and the gearing of success to this fulfillment. Because of this diminishing lack, the tendency in our movement is to break into smaller pieces of self-isolating community that are motivated by common interest issues.

This tendency to fracture into isolated parts is further compounded by the absence of a commonly accepted sense of religious mission that could, potentially, overcome the aforementioned lack of unifying forces and transcendently establish a bonding beyond fragility. This traffics on some of the laws that govern institutional power. At the heart of these laws is the force of commonality. While diversity may enrich internal relationships and provoke toward openness, it is only commonality that induces profound community and produces sufficient power to impact the social order toward constructive transformation. If there is a lesson of history that will not be denied, this is it. It seems apparent that it has been a long time since Unitarian Universalism expressed such profoundness of community and such social power.

This skewed institutionalism has caused us to convert the dynamics that actually make for social power into dysfunctional distortions. An expressed perceptual example of this distortion is the notion that unity exists in diversity. There is no social dynamic that supports this contention other than desire for it to be so. The social truth is the opposite, namely, that diversity exists in unity. Or, to say this differently, it is unity that permits diversity to flourish without destructive effect. The consequence of such skewing is that instead of being a whole comprised of supportive parts, we are more of a conglomerate of parts forever seeking a supportive wholeness but with little satisfying success.

This lack of unifying forces and this skewing of institutional dynamics makes for social impotence. And there is only one antidote. This antidote is an investment in the fulfillment of a common sense of religious mission that can bond our disparate parts into a unity of wholeness. If we wish for any capacity to motivate in a deliberate fashion toward social empowerment, then this investment in a sense of common mission is the only sustaining source. We simply have no other alternative if we want to move past our primary focus of internalized ministry to individuals toward an externalized ministry that engages the world in a transforming manner.

As a total religious movement, whatever social power we have will be commensurate with this sensing and investing in a common sense of religious mission. And as individual congregations, whatever motivation can be mustered to deal with needed transition will traffic on this sensing and investing.

Overcoming Obstacles

Given an understanding of the issues involved in making the transition from a Pastoral Congregation to a Program Congregation, several questions arise. How is it possible to overcome the potential obstacles and institute the many facets of this transition? How is it possible to motivate a congregation toward effecting this transition? After all, it seems to be such a huge task that requires a lot of resource investment.

Whatever the obstacles, the answer to these questions is a revitalized sense of the congregation's religious mission. Given all the lacks previously mentioned, there is not a single aspect of this transition that does not rely on the motivation of insight and resources that only a strong sense of religious mission can both generate and sustain. If this is already extant in congregational life then all that is required is consciousness raising, a game plan, and commitment. If it is not, then, this is the place to start.

Even if there is a perceptual understanding of the nature of the transition and a game plan to implement it, if there is no motivating and engaging sense of mission the battle will normally be uphill, energy draining and ultimately discouraging. Moreover, private agenda will invade the process and implementation will be skewed, and much may have to be undone that gets done.

It is not enough to say that the congregation has a mission statement. Many congregations have them. There are three questions that follow. The first is whether or not this statement is simply a listing of facets of ministry that fall out of mission or a statement of mission, itself. The second is whether or not this statement is actually motivating the congregation's resource commitments toward fulfillment. And the third is whether this is a religious mission or some other mission.

Thus, it makes little difference that a congregation has a mission statement if it is uninspiring and does not motivate toward its own fulfillment or is not kin to the institution's reason for being. In any of these cases, the question is "Why?" and the answer to the question must be addressed in some way that provides a religious mission statement that does inspire and motivate the congregation as a whole. And that which inspires and motivates is that which has become owned. So the ultimate issue becomes ownership of this statement. And aside from education and the craft of the statement, itself, nothing instills a sense of ownership like actual participation in the statement's construction. Thus, revisiting the process of construction may become a revitalizing activity.

Sometimes long-term members will resist the idea of revisiting the notion of mission and, particularly, the notion of developing a new mission-covenant statement. Often this resistance is rooted in their fusion of a certain past statement and a period of excitement and growth when that statement was being used. It is difficult for them to see that this past statement may hold no clarity of purpose or inspiration for newer members of the congregation who did not experience this past period of excitement. And they will suggest that all that is necessary is to resurrect this statement even though it may not have served its purpose for a number of years.

If these are influential leaders it is important to convince them of the value of a process that engages the congregation in developing a new statement of religious mission so that a new spirit of ownership and inspiration rises in congregational life. Mission statements are geared to certain dominating perspectives in a congregation's life and to language useful during that period of time. Five, fifteen, or twenty-five years later the perspectives may no longer dominate and the language may no longer be useful. Evolution takes its toll on such statements. The wise congregation understands this and is sensitive to the need to use both ownership process and new language to revitalize its sense of religious mission.

The power of a mission statement that promotes a keen sense of religious mission cannot be underestimated in giving impetus toward making a congenial and energy-saving transition from a Pastoral Congregation to a Program Congregation. It is the key.

Having stated this, there is a proviso. If the excitement of human transformation is not taking place alongside the emphasis on the congregation's religious mission, then there is no psychological relationship between the statement and significant happening. Actually fulfilling the statement is as important as having it. The power to captivate attention and devotion lies within empowering the statement with its own effect.

9

Transition and Control

Picasso suggested that every act of creation is first of all an act of destruction. This picture of creation and destruction happening together in a rather chaotic state is an apt metaphor of the transition period between being a Pastoral Congregation and becoming a Program Congregation. More than anything else it is a state of flux during which the old is passing away and the new is coming into being.

Such instability in institutional life gives birth to opportunity. Thus, a transition is a time of creativity. It is a time for shaping that which will define and determine the future. However, when the uncertainty of flux sets in, the first reaction of many members will be that of loathing and fear. The loathing will be over the loss of the security of stability and the comfort of the familiar. This will translate into a sense of lack of control that easily converts into a fear of the unknown and the new. Any major transition will be subject to this response of loathing and fear.

If the transition is to be successful, then leadership must help people direct their energies from loathing and fear to excitement and anticipation. The excitement is about being able to create and shape a new future. The anticipation is of the rewards that await this new future. This refocusing of energies is, in reality, a shift from being out of control to being in control.

Many members will find this paradox difficult to grasp. They will assume that the sense of loss that generates their fear equates to loss of control. It is the old issue of whether the glass is half empty or half full. Thus, what members need to be led to understand is that control, in respect to institutional life, lies far less in the chaotic nature of transition and far more in the state of mind members assume toward this chaos. In brief, members choose whether they will be in control or out of control by whether they decide to focus their energy of response on fearing the chaos or anticipating the opportunity, by loathing over what will be lost or by exciting over what will be gained.

Naming the losses and envisioning the gains can help members shift their attitudes toward the joy of control. As a Chinese proverb asserts: "The beginning of wisdom is to call things by their right names."

It is also true that while all transition is change not all change is transition. Change is only transition when it leads to investment in a new model of reality. The negative energy of loathing and fear is a response to the confrontation with the symptoms of transition that retards the possibilities of that transition. The positive energy of excitement and anticipation is a response to the confrontation with the symptoms of transition that facilitates the possibilities of that transition.

The difference between these two responses is analogous to a horse exerting its energies in balking at the direction given by the rein of change or permitting its energies to flow in the reining direction of change. Balking is energy spent in the inertia of stasis while permission is energy harnessed to the movement of direction.

Whatever measure of control a congregation is able to exert over the Pastoral to Program Congregation transition will be in direct proportion to the amount of energy members exert away from loathing and fear and toward excitement and anticipation.

10

Settlement Pitfalls

In the transition from a Pastoral to a Program Congregation, there are pitfalls that await both congregation and minister in the process of settling new professional leadership on the parish field. In either case, being enticed into one of these pits will prove harmful or disastrous. The way to avoid this possibility is to remain aware of the presence of these pitfalls and do those things necessary to refuse their invitation.

The Congregation

A significant percentage of congregations seeking new ministers will be involved in this shift from a Pastoral to a Program culture. For those congregations thus involved, the actual activities of this process of seeking and Calling a minister constitutes a pitfall. Here is how stumbling into the pit happens. The congregation is unaware of not only the dynamics of the shift but also unaware that it is involved in these dynamics. In brief, a shift is either occurring or must occur for it to continue growing and having an effective ministry but neither of these facts are part of the congregation's framework of reality.

Because of this unawareness, the congregation will tend to invest the transactions of calling a minister with pastoral perspectives. This means it will look for a minister who

+ is strongly committed to the ministry of pastoral care
+ is warm, embracing, and personable and manifests a caring and compassionate spirit
+ is open to sharing those personal revelations that invite depth of friendship with all members of the congregation
+ is capable of offering adult religious education experiences that enhance congregant-minister relationships and invite membership growth
+ is reasonably good at church administration.

Normally, it will not place as high a priority on those attributes that empower ministerial leadership in a Program Congregation such as

+ big picture perspective
+ worship-crafting capacities
+ facilitation abilities
+ institutional wisdom
+ inspiring leadership
+ training skills.

A principle that governs institutional life is that leadership makes everything happen that's going to happen. Thus, if a congregation that is involved in a Pastoral to Program shift Calls a minister with Pastoral Congregation perspectives and skills it has, ipso facto, committed to remaining a Pastoral Congregation. This is so, irrespective of its levels of awareness in respect to the nature of this shift. The pit has beckoned and the congregation has succumbed.

Unfortunately, this seems to be a counterproductive behavior on the part of many congregations either in the midst of this shift or on the verge of this shift. It is one of the primary reasons why congregations tend to languish in plateau stuckness for excessive spans of time. The tragedy is that most congregations who have fallen into this pit intuitively know that something is wrong but do not have the appropriate language and perspective tools to empower an exit into a different future. Being unable to name the problem they cannot name the solution.

It must also be acknowledged that this same pit beckons a congregation when the Pastoral to Program shift has been identified as the necessity of institutional effectiveness and the membership, still enamored of the Pastoral style of professional ministry, Calls a minister with primarily pastoral qualities, despite this identification.

The Minister

A minister who accepts the Call of a congregation that is involved in this shift but is unaware of its involvement is susceptible to at least two major pitfalls. Both have to do with the minister's own leadership.

The first pitfall traffics on a match that cannot go beyond its limits. If the minister is a skilled pastoral leader and engages the congregation toward success, then, unless some peculiar circumstance prohibits, this very success will cause membership growth. If this pastoral focus persists, the congregation is most likely to arrive at a threshold of numerical and dynamic possibility for this kind of leadership and plateau in membership growth. If the relationship between the congregation and minister remains stable it will stagnate in this plateau. The limit of this style of ministerial leadership is the pitfall and the plateau is its beckoning for the minister to invite the congregation to become a permanent resident.

The second leadership pitfall has to do with a potential mismatch between Pastoral Congregation expectations and Program Congregation skills. Assume that, by either deliberate vision or unintended good fortune, a Pastoral Congregation involved in this shift calls a minister with Program Congregation skills. And assume that this skill set, as is often the case, does not include a strong propensity toward pastoral care or an embracing gregariousness of spirit. Even so, the congregation may have exactly what it needs by way of ministerial leadership skills to become successful in its shift to a Program Congregation culture. Despite this possibility, the minister's leadership can easily be sabotaged by resistant members who are unwilling to let loose of Pastoral Congregation expectations.

Here is how it could happen. Those who wish a personal relationship of friendship with the new minister "just as they had with the last minister" will judge the new minister on the basis of this expectation. If this expectation is not fulfilled the most likely scenario to follow will be a campaign to diminish the minister's power. This normally begins with complaints about the minister's lack of warmth and friendliness and progresses to charges of "deliberate slights" and ultimately may degenerate into aspersions that imply that the minister is the enemy of those things that are dear and sacred to the beloved community. Those involved in this attempt to disqualify ministerial leadership are not evil people. They are laity whose dashed expectations have reduced their taste for professional leadership to bitterness. It is a taste produced by the conflicts of mismatch.

This progression that seems to be an attack on the integrity of the minister is the pitfall that invites combat. This combat will most likely be engaged by the minister who

- ✦ does not recognize the nature and meaning of what is transpiring and, thus, assumes the issue is personal

- does not seek to diffuse the potential harm in as professional a manner as possible, thus, assumes a reaction of indignation and defensiveness
- does not lead the congregation to take ownership of the real issues, thus, assumes the sacrificial posture of the messianic figure
- does not acknowledge the commitment depth of lay leadership, thus, dismisses the possibilities of redemption and change.

The tragedy of falling into and dwelling in this pit is that it reduces the issue of the conflict to a level of imperceptiveness that can have no outcome except loss for all that are involved.

Conclusion

For both congregation and minister, wisdom dictates an immunity to these traps through an imbued awareness of the dynamics of the Pastoral to Program shift that makes the ministerial search process a deliberate matchmaking endeavor.

11

Trust and the Shift

As a congregation moves toward completing this shift from a Pastoral to a Program Congregation, certain issues of concern may arise. One of these issues is trust. In the Pastoral Congregation members expect to be included in most important decision-making processes. This expectation is an expression of an inclusive spirit of community that often takes on sacrosanct qualities in the Pastoral Congregation. Moreover, because of this sense of ownership there is usually a tendency for decision-making processes to become occasions for congregational micromanagement. However, as a congregation grows into Program attendance size, this kind of decision-making participation significantly diminishes institutional effectiveness.

The operative institutional principle that governs this diminishment is that the larger a congregation grows the more imperative becomes small group and rapid process decision making. Otherwise, the institution becomes a captive of the process, itself, and decisions that could be made easily become mired within this process. In turn, the machinery of effectiveness can be slowed to a crawl.

A congregation seeking to escape this ineffectiveness will be forced by the operative institutional principle to streamline its decision-making processes. Out of the tension between this streamlining and the retained expectation of members to be included in the processes tends to flow the possibility of distrust. Essentially, this distrust is a fear of the loss of that sense of control that has been produced by prior heavy decision-making participation.

Such distrust, born of this fear, is endemic to views of inclusiveness that traffic on a deep devotion to democratic principles. This notion of inclusiveness is vital to the community spirit of the Pastoral Congregation and is, thus, understandable. However, the notion of inclusiveness is also vital to the community spirit of the Program Congregation. But this spirit of inclusiveness and the membership decision-making micromanagement typical of the Pastoral Congregation are not viewed as synonymous. It is this false synonymity that often feeds a spirit of distrust in the shift to Program Congregation status.

Suspicions about the role of authority figures in the Unitarian Universalist religious experience sometimes enter into the issue of trust. In the Pastoral Congregation, a strange phenomenon occurs. Irrespective of such suspicions, the minister is gifted with a rather profound authority with which the congregation is quite comfortable. Nurturing this gift of authority is a trust that is grounded in the level of friendship the minister normally has with congregants and the deep connections fostered through the ministry of pastoral care.

The community life of the congregation revolves around and thrives on this authority-trust relationship. An important part of this authority has to do with the minister making administrative decisions vital to the congregation's ministry. It is how a great deal of the work gets done despite the congregation's orientation toward micromanagement. It is one of the basic characteristics of the lifestyle of the Pastoral Congregation and is part of the community's way of being that is similar to the relationship of trusted authority a loving parental figure has with the rest of a family unit.

However, when the congregation grows too large for this friendship-ministry-trust basis for ministerial authority to be nurtured and sustained, it dissipates and issues about authority and trust can take on a different focus. Once, the congregation could trust the minister to make vital decisions but now they do not have the kind of relationship that fosters such trust. The Pastoral Congregation, made possible by the peculiarities of its attendance size, has disappeared and, along with it, its unique ground of trust-building relationships. So, segments of the laity may begin to wish for more complete ownership of the decision-making processes as a way of warding off the negative images they carry that are associated with the denial of democracy in ecclesiastical forms of religion.

With this growth into largeness the congregation begins trafficking on the dynamics of the Program Congregation. There are two primary differences from the Pastoral Congregation relative to the issues of trust, authority, and inclusion in decision making. One is that the Program Congregation does not usually, ipso facto, endow its minister with special authority. The minister is viewed as a mentor but must prove to be so in earning the trust of the congregation, and this trust has to do with wisdom and skills.

The other difference is that while the Pastoral Congregation's relationship with the minister allows for a concentration of trust-authority, the size and complexity of the Program Congregation precludes such trust-enhancing relationships. Moreover, the authority to make decisions is spread out in an agreed-upon division of responsibilities between laity and minister based on the nature of the various facets of the congregation's ministry. Thus, the kind of relationship that enhances trust in this division of responsibilities, of necessity, is a spirit and behavior of partnership with its focus on mutual empowerment.

In brief, in the Program Congregation two things happen. First, the processes of decision making spread out in a complex web of authority that is not easily engaged in reference to trust. The lack of simplicity of this complex web denies the inclusive approach typical of the Pastoral Congregation. And, second, the dynamics of leadership relationships and organizational structures divests the congregation of a clear singular locus of authority. What does exist is more of a diffused nexus of various authorities that involve all the basic lay and professional leadership of the congregation who share in its responsibility, maintenance, and enhancement.

Essentially, everything changes in respect to the culture of decision making that exists in the Pastoral to Program shift because the basic cultures of these two congregational attendance-size types are radically different. This cultural shift involves every primary institutional component: organization, inclusion, community atmosphere, ministerial relationships, authority, responsibilities, the role of the laity, complexity, decision making, and focus of ministry. For those with a Pastoral Congregation mentality, this creates a mystifying distance and complexity of authority locus between themselves and the decision-making process. And this may either create or further enhance a personal sense of not being in control and, thus, a not-included-distrust. Consequently, all of those things the leadership of a Program Congregation does to streamline decision making for the sake of effective ministry is easily viewed with a suspicion born of such not-in-control-not-included distrust.

The forgoing represent possibilities of attitude and response based on the unique characteristics of Pastoral and Program Congregation models. The analysis is not intended as a template that must be imposed on the circumstance of congregations making this shift. Whatever the degree that any of these possibilities find expression in the life of a congregation involved in this shift depends on its history, the peculiar qualities of its membership makeup, its unique culture, and where it might be within the scope of the shift process.

For example, a congregation may have been going through this process of transition for many years in a fashion unaware of what has been happening and why a level of ineffectiveness has existed in its ministry. Upon becoming aware of the nature and state of the congregation within this shift, it might discover that the negative trust issues that a congregation new to the shift might experience does not exist in their ministry life. Congregations should ascertain where they are in the process, acknowledge their successes, and move on with completing the transition.

When making major institutional changes, such as this shift, the sense of the institution's stability may seem to soften and such can add to anxiety levels about being out of control relative to decision making. Everything that the leadership of the congregation can do to firm up this sense of stability, reduce levels of anxiety, and address the trust issues inherent in the shift is imperative to keeping the available energy from being drained away from affecting the shift. Following are some suggestions designed to aid in this leadership effort.

1. The sooner and more fully the leadership of a congregation that is involved in this shift understands its dynamics and has the language to articulate its meanings, the more readily they will take ownership of either making the shift happen or completing it. Initiating a program of education becomes a key to success in this respect.

Kicking off such an educational process with a major all-congregation retreat with an agenda that gets at these dynamics and applies them to the congregation's present status will greatly facilitate this ownership. The more people feel included in analyzing the congregation's status and projecting its needs, the greater the possibility of that kind of ownership that invests positive energy toward future fulfillment.

2. The shift to a Program Congregation, of necessity, includes a corresponding shift in the manner of governance. The requirement is that the decision-making process be honed into more efficient increments such as individuals and small groups with the authority to process decisions in a timely fashion. With this creation of complexity and diffusion of focus in decision making, issues of trust can emerge. This means that leadership must be deliberate in its attempts to enhance the level of trust in this different way of making decisions. One of the pervasive ways this goal can be accomplished is to make sure that the basis of all such decision making is driven by policy. Such a policy orientation facilitates trust because:

    +   It makes possible the gearing of all decisions to the fulfillment of the congregation's Mission-Covenant.
    +   It reflects the ingenuity of commonly held wisdom and tends to be more readily accepted as community norms.
    +   It levels the ground of decision making through its impartial regulation of the behavior of all members, staff and ministers.
    +   It serves as a gauge for constraint, judgment, and action.

+ It is a set of public guidelines to which all members are privy and thus discourages the application of private agenda in decision making.

+ It gives uniform guidance and wisdom to the management of conflicts in congregational life.

+ It infers mutual empowerment.

3. Leadership can give devotion to making and modeling decisions grounded in the conviction that "power shared is power multiplied." Such devotion and modeling speaks to a commitment to the congregation's mission and ministry as the first priority in decision making and diminishes possible untrusting suspicions about private motivations.

4. Leadership can begin all relationships based on the attitude that people, whatever their status, will be trusted to fulfill their responsibilities to the best of their abilities and must evidence a pattern of violation before trust becomes an issue. This assumes that when leadership is elected or appointed it is done so with a view of credentials of trust.

5. Leadership can commit to and hold high the functions of a Committee On Ministry that is based on a workable model of that concept. A well-designed Committee On Ministry that is led by laypeople of stature can effectively deal with most issues of trust that arise in congregational life and greatly facilitate the congregation's trust level.

6. By whatever name it may be called, the group that is responsible for nominating lay leadership can place trust-

worthiness at the top of its list of criteria for selection. This is particularly important during a time of transition that is characterized by the instability of change and, thus, makes the institution susceptible to issues of distrust. The warm body approach to the selection of leadership is usually counterproductive within itself, let alone during a time that demands trust, skill, and wisdom.

7. It is also obvious that a congregation that might be calling a minister during this shift process must take care that the ability to enhance trust be a serious criteria of this professional leadership. Some awareness of the dynamics of the shift from a Pastoral to a Program Congregation is an element that will encourage the membership to express this confidence of trust. Exploring the trust history of ministerial candidates should be a serious endeavor and such exploration should go well beyond those references provided by the candidate.

Trust is a critical issue in energy investment, honesty expression, and community building. And, at no time is it more vitalizing than when the congregation is involved in change. Since leadership makes everything happen that's going to happen, then it becomes responsible for creating an atmosphere of trust in the congregation's ministry. And it must take special care in this area when the congregation is making the shift from the Pastoral to Program mode. People are most apt to engage the creative possibilities inherent in change within an atmosphere of community safety. Expressing trust and a sense of safety are mutually enhancing.

12

Form and Process Synergism

The shift from a Pastoral to a Program Congregation is a holistic drama. The Pastoral Congregation and the Program Congregation are different systems reflecting different approaches to mission fulfillment. These approaches are dictated not only by attendance size but also by the differing dynamics of simplicity and complexity of their respective makeup and what they need in professional leadership. And, as with all systems, when there is a systemic shift of major parts all of the other parts that make up the whole must be brought into harmony if there is to be maximum synergistic power. Otherwise, energy expressions become counterproductive and ineffectiveness ensues. Following are some of those facets of ministry that have an important role in this harmony alignment.

Congregational Retreat

It is the custom of most Pastoral Congregations to have an annual board of trustees retreat to meld into a leadership team and establish a vision for the immediate future of the congregation.

Because of the community dynamics of the Pastoral Congregation its board is generally viewed as the basic leadership body of the congregation. And many such boards are actually

constructed to represent the various facets of the congregation's ministry. As previously suggested, it is not uncommon for
these boards to incorporate the functions of not only a board
but also a program council and a finance committee. So, when
the board has an annual retreat to plan for the future, the basic
ministry facets of the congregation are usually represented.

This is not the case in an effectively organized Program
Congregation. For effectiveness, attendance size requires a multiplicity of leadership beyond the board because of the proliferation of programs and the leadership demands of these
programs. Continued growth demands more ministers and
staff and lay leadership and a clearer delineation of responsibility between facets of ministry under the guidance of these
ministers, staff, and lay leadership. The result is a complex
web of both lay and professional leadership. And even if the
Program Congregation's board is organized around a Pastoral
Congregation model, this ministry representation will not
overcome the problems of this complexity or the issue of its
multiplicity of leaders.

When a board decides to move to a policy governance model
it further divests itself of specified representation of ministry
facets. This divestiture requires even more leadership outside
the board. Although this leadership is connected to the board
through mission and policy, it is self-driven. Thus, an even
greater delineation is created between the leadership facets of
ministry and the board.

But whether the governance of the board is by a traditional
model or a policy governance model, the question is the same:
"What does this movement from simplicity to complexity in
leadership proliferation have to do with the board's annual
retreat?" The answer is that it calls for a different view of the
retreat's makeup and purpose. This does not mean that the

board cannot have a retreat for its own purposes without the attendance of the rest of the congregation's leadership.

However, if the board wishes the more extensive leadership of the Program Congregation to feel itself as part of a team and to imbibe of those visions that will instruct the congregation's future, then it must have an annual retreat that includes this leadership. And if it does not make this shift in perspective it will find its time and energies being consumed by the necessity of inviting this leadership into a team spirit and enlisting this leadership to own the visions the board has created. Moreover, it may double its energy and time output in trying to accomplish this task and still not be successful. In brief, the board of a Program Congregation, acting alone as a leadership team, will only increase its own workload.

The reason for this conclusion is that leaders who have not been invited into the team and who have not been privy to the creation of visions are far less likely to feel valued as part of a team or take ownership of the visions the board proposes. Thus, not including all of the basic leaders of a Program Congregation in an annual leadership retreat may even, inadvertently, foster independent attitudes and visions on the part of these leaders that could actually be in contention with those of the board. The point is that, without a leadership retreat that puts all the congregation's leaders on the same page, the board has bought itself an enormous amount of extra work.

Whatever has been said about including the congregation's leadership applies equally to the entire congregation. The larger the number of congregants attending such a retreat, the broader the possibilities of ownership and support of the conclusions and visions reached during the retreat. Moreover, an entire congregational retreat may generate much needed leadership for the fulfillment of the visions that emerge from the retreat. So, while the board may invest extra time and energy in being sure that the congregation's basic leadership attends this retreat, it may wish to also encourage the attendance of every member as an act of commitment to the congregation's future and as a possible enlistment of new leadership enamored of the visions created at this event.

Here is the principle: In a Program Congregation, the smaller the body inviting a team spirit and creating a vision for the whole, the greater the time and energy required to enlist the rest of the congregation. Here is the principle in reverse: The larger the body inviting a team spirit and creating a vision for the whole, the less the time and energy required to enlist the rest of the congregation.

Office Manager (Administrator)

The Pastoral Congregation normally gets by with an administrator taking care of those things unattended by the minister. Since the ministry of the congregation revolves around the minister's presence and power, the administrator can usually take care of the details of running the institution if the various committees are functioning with effectiveness.

With the shift to a program focus the Program Congregation has grown too complex for this minimalist approach to administration. Not only will it need a competent office manager, it will eventually need an assistant to this manager. Among the many reasons for this need for additional office personnel are:

- ✦   As professional, staff, and lay leadership grow in size, so do their administrative needs and the material required to fuel their various programs.
- ✦   Communications become primary to success, and the congregation's office is the hub of all such activity.

+ For effectiveness, the congregation's newsletter will need to be an office responsibility, whether it is edited and printed within the office or not.

+ As programs grow so do space needs and, consequently, the assignment of space to varied groups becomes a key aspect of office management.

+ If the congregation rents its facility to outside groups, this may become a time-consuming aspect of administration.

+ There needs to be some day-to-day locus for building management and maintenance that cannot be fulfilled effectively by lay leadership whose primary investments are elsewhere.

+ Custodial personnel need to be supervised.

+ Certain financial aspects of institutional life need to be cared for in the office.

+ If the congregation has moved into a policy governance model the executive team will need administrative support.

+ Someone needs to be able to care for the details while the manager deals with the big picture.

Essentially, a congregation whose ministry has expanded to a program focus will generate a high level of administrative need to keep things running smoothly. The Program Congregation that wishes an effective ministry must have an effective office administration. Because this administration has grown complex beyond the Pastoral Congregation's model and involves components of oversight that are well beyond the simplicities of administration, the more appropriate term of office manager best describes the role. Thus, the Program Congregation must bite the bullet and hire sufficient management, administrative staff and appropriate up-to-date equipment to make this happen. There is no effective substitute. Outdated equipment only draws down on more of the time and resources of the office team.

Milestones/Joys and Concerns

Many Pastoral Congregations have a fondness for that ritual that happens during the Sunday worship service generally called by such euphemisms as Milestones or Joys and Concerns. This is a typical focus of a community-oriented congregation. It has to do with celebrating and fostering that sense of family connection where everybody knows what is happening with everybody else and where a mutually affirming and mutually embracing atmosphere is essential to the well-being of community.

In reality, it is a ritual that most graphically characterizes the perspectives of the smallest in size attendance of religious communities, the Family Congregation. It appeals to the Pastoral Congregation because it is generally working hard at not losing its sense of family as its community grows. And it usually survives in the Pastoral Congregation because it so dramatically symbolizes the family orientation of mutual interest and concern that has been dear to those who where a part of the Family Congregation out of which it has grown. Moreover, during the worship service it dramatizes the spirit of community that is at the heart of the Pastoral Congregation's celebration of its own being.

Because of the multi-celled nature and need dynamics of the Program Congregation, retaining this ritual in the worship experience seems more a nostalgia trip for members who cling to the community drama of the Pastoral Congregation than it is a prerequisite for effective worship. Indeed, it may well be a drawback to completing the shift from a Pastoral to a Program

Congregation because it keeps a focus on time past, a small attendance-size perspective, and fosters the illusion that nothing about the nature of community has changed.

The question is why people seem so protective about the retention of this ritual in a congregation where attendance size divests it of either sense or practicality. One reason may be that the congregation's sense of religious mission, that is the primary bonding agent for all its facets of ministry as well as its members, is so low it fails to offer meaningful connection or participatory nobility. Thus, members grasp for any substitute, howsoever symbolic it may be.

Another reason that traffics on this propensity to substitute is that the congregation may not offer small group ministries that afford people an opportunity to share their deepest concerns and relate through a profound community connection. As long as there are no strong motivations and experiences that bind people in common purpose and humanness there will be the tendency to substitute form for substance and invest in symbolic activities.

Still another reason is that it symbolizes the spirit of the typical Pastoral Congregation worship experience and some people are unwilling to let loose of this symbolism even though it might have little appeal to most members. It may be that such irrelevant rituals have enabled some to actually make the shift. That is, they will go along with the shift as long as they can bring some of their favorite symbols of the past into the present.

There are at least five essential problems in retaining this ritual in the Program Congregation. First, relationships are normally stretched so thin in this congregation's attendance size that most of the milestones shared will not facilitate any sense of real community because there will be no valid connections to make that possible. Second, even though some of

what is shared may be profound, the tendency is toward trivial-
izing the focus of this sharing in the interest of adult show-and-
tell. Third, the average participant exerts little time discipline
over the length of their sharing and the larger the congregation
grows the more serious becomes this problem. Fourth, people
constantly take advantage of the opportunity to make veiled
announcements rather than sharing milestones and to introduce
guests as if their visits were, indeed, life milestones. Because
of these problems, many attending, and particularly guests, will
often express negative comments about this element.

A last and vital problem relates to the burden of challenge,
growth, inspiration, and motivation that the Sunday worship
service plays in the larger Program Congregation. In order for
this experience to fulfill the expectations of this burden, it must
move step by step toward the possibility of transformation.
Thus, it must be carefully planned and executed with a timed
discipline. It is this planning and discipline that is key to its
power. This throwback ritual not only takes away vital minutes
that could be devoted to empowering this experience, its abuse
can easily obviate all the careful planning and discipline exerted
to make the time of worship a powerful experience for the total
gathered community.

One of the criteria for the inclusion of any element into the
worship experience is that it has the potential of appealing to
the total of those present. Once a congregation has reached the
attendance size of the Program Congregation, it is no longer
possible for elements like Milestones/Joys and Concerns to
qualify when applying this criterion. Such elements can only
appeal to a limited number of people.

When a minister, for whatever reasons, decides to delete this
ritual from the worship agenda, this decision will often become
a lightning rod for all manner of other member dissatisfac-

tions. This happens because many member dissatisfactions are sometimes vague or unwarranted and the concrete nature of this ritual provides a container for the emotional content of the anger behind all such dissatisfactions. This tends to contaminate the real issue and make any kind of reasonable dialogue almost impossible with those who have a strong attachment to the ritual.

Family and Pastoral Congregation devotees may even launch an attack on the minister challenging his/her right to tamper with "a sacred ritual affirmed by the congregation as essential to its community spirit." The chief complaint may be that the deletion was made without consulting the membership and therefore constitutes authoritarian behavior foreign to the democratic spirit. Some laity, with essential Pastoral Congregation perspectives, because of their proneness toward viewing consensus as the only legitimate means of making decisions about critical community issues, may assume that the ritual content of the worship experience should be under their control. Such complaints raise serious issues about Freedom of the Pulpit that may need to be addressed in some satisfactory manner by congregations involved in dialogue about this ritual.

A Program Congregation that deletes this ritual and wishes a powerful and inclusive worship experience will need to figure out how to deal with the deficits this deletion appears to represent and how to engage those illusions that the ritual has fostered about attendance dynamics and the sense of congregational community.

However, for those enamored of what this ritual symbolizes, nothing may be viewed as a satisfactory substitute and no amount of logic will be persuasive in respect to its omission from the worship experience. And it is possible that some of these people will fight every move to make the shift from a

Pastoral Congregation to a Program Congregation despite what the rest of the membership may desire because they will, at heart, forever remain advocates of the Pastoral Congregation's dynamics even when those dynamics have long disappeared. That is, they will expend their energies fighting for institutional ways of being that no longer exist because their lifestyle is geared to a past that no longer exists. And there seems to be a percentage of every congregation's membership that is devoted to engaging such an irrelevant lifestyle.

Social Action

There are two primary ways by which our congregations tend to approach social action. One is to seek to honor everybody's individual concerns and focus on a multiplicity of social issues. This requires dividing the available energy and money and doing whatever can be done with the amount allotted to each issue. An apt metaphor for this approach is the shotgun blast where the multiple pellets represent given amounts of energy and money propelled toward a wide variety of concerns with hopes that something might happen. While this approach normally does not seem to make any discernable long-term impact on the issues involved, it does allow those with favored projects to feel that the congregation is addressing their individual concerns.

The other approach is to determine a single social issue and propel all available energy and money toward its resolution. An apt metaphor is a rifle shot where one pellet of significant size is carefully aimed at one concern. In this approach there is the potential of making some long-term impact due to carefully aimed significant resources. Moreover, while this focus does not permit everyone's individual concerns to be addressed, if selected carefully, it does make possible the participation of multiple age groups in the selected project. Thus, it has the potential of becoming a total religious community effort that bonds the membership in common purpose as well as addressing a common social concern. Because of its encompassing nature, some congregations label this approach an All Church Project.

The larger a congregation grows in attendance the more it becomes apparent that the shotgun approach to social action can only satisfy the concerns of a few people and, as a rule, can only address social symptoms. On the other hand, the rifle approach's singular focus can bring satisfaction to the entire congregation and may have sufficient energy and money behind it to potentially deal with social cause.

While the shotgun approach feeds the spirit of individualism and acknowledges variety, the rifle approach feeds the spirit of community and acknowledges commonality. Since one of the most profound needs of the Program Congregation is for community bonding and its resources permit an effective addressing of social causes, it may wish to consider which of these two approaches best addresses both its internal and external ministries. That is, it may wish to consider which of these approaches is most harmonious with it attendance size, facilitates a common bonding and adds the greatest social power to its synergistic potential.

Communications

Making the transition to a Program Congregation requires adequate resources. This means taking a hard look at staff, program, and equipment needs and costs. For many congregations, this hard look is through the eyes of resource scarcity rather than resource abundance. The usual approach to the budget issues that normally ensue from this scarcity mentality is to look for ways to cut the cost of ministry in some areas in order to raise the cost of ministry in other areas (as opposed to increasing the pledge level so that all ministry needs can be addressed).

As a rule, one of those areas chosen to cut is communications. This is an easy choice since the "savings" can be measured rather precisely. And this normally means reducing the number of times the congregation's newsletter is sent out. But such is self-defeating because the principle operating in the decision is that the larger a congregation grows in its membership the greater is its need for focused and timely communications.

The view that communications is secondary in importance to other ministry needs tends to be a heritage of Pastoral Congregation experience. In the Pastoral Congregation gossip generally plays a vital role in communications. There is an expectation that people will just know what is going on because of interpersonal communication. To be effective, such gossip depends on two factors. One is the existence of relational networks. The other is a sense of family motivation in communication. The attendance size of the Program Congregation is beyond either of these factors and its communications must, therefore, be deliberate. Its relational networks must be tied together in mutuality through the system of communications, itself. And its motivation must be generated with deliberateness because only a few people in the Program Congregation will show up for events just to experience being part of the community.

There is also a communications issue of specificity in the Program Congregation. Members of the Pastoral Congregation will attend the weekly worship services because the community is gathering to celebrate its existence. It does not make a great deal of difference what the title or nature of the service might be because such is secondary to motivation for attendance. On the other hand, if such appeal for attendance exists in the Program Congregation, it is minimal. The theme and nature of the service take on great significance as a motivating factor in attendance. It assures members that attending the service is more important to their well-being than all the other options that are crying for their attention (coffee and the *New York Times*, hiking, lolling around, catching up on "whatever," etc.). Thus, it becomes imperative that this information be placed before members constantly as a motivating factor in their attendance. This imperativeness is further accentuated because of the low motivational factor religious mission normally plays in the institutional life of a Unitarian Universalist congregation.

Here is the issue for the Program Congregation. There must be a pervasive system of communication that motivates participation and reminds of meetings and events in a timely manner or its program will suffer and its support will diminish. To be pervasive, every member must be part of the network. To motivate, the communication must announce quality and enhance appetite. To be timely, the communication must be calendar sensitive. Only a weekly newsletter is capable of fulfilling all of these criteria simultaneously. How this calendar gets distributed is a different issue. With today's technology it is possible to become creative about the means of distribution. The limitation is that all members do not have access to this technology and many of those who do are often too busy to access it with timely consistency.

But the issue is deeper than just pervasiveness, motivation, timeliness, and means. The production of the newsletter, itself, is a message. What articles are given prime space, how well they are written to motivate, and their length are critical. If it is quality that is being announced as motivation then the first statement of quality is the quality of the announcement. Thus, editing becomes a critical priority.

The competition for the time and commitment of the Program Congregation's members is fierce, multiple, and daily. Only weekly qualitative reminders of what, when, where, and why can expect to address this competition with any hope of profound success. So, the Program Congregation cannot allow itself to fall into the oxymoronic trap of reducing the communications upon which its very success depends.

Community Events

While the Pastoral Congregation is small enough for most of its events to draw a sizable portion of its membership into attendance, that is not the case with the Program Congregation. The Program Congregation must be deliberate in its attempt to maintain the spirit of community for a membership so large that its constant tendency is to fragment into unbonded parts. While the Sunday worship and educational experience is critical to providing a spiritual glue that denies this fragmenting tendency, it is insufficient within itself to do so because of its very nature, focus, and time restraints.

There must be events that are more specifically focused on bonding through other means than worship. And many of these events must be intergenerational in character in order to honor the congregation's need for family inclusion. An All Church Retreat is an example. But there also need to be events with an adult focus of less time duration than a family retreat. There seems to be no common wisdom about the number of these but I would suggest a minimum of three or four spread throughout the church year that are so compelling in focus, are so well planned and executed, and have such a positive impact that they inspire enduring congregation-wide commitment.

The conclusion is that the Program Congregation needs to plan a series of annual events (aside from the weekly worship and educational experience), both intergenerational and adult, that invite the congregational membership to experience what it means to be a whole community. Such experiences are important for they remind members that the whole is larger than its parts. This reminder reinforces the notion that the parts participate within a grander nobility beyond themselves.

Symbolic Tokenism

Pastoral Congregations are prone to carry their single cell Family Congregation background into their entire existence, including their growth into a Program Congregation. That is, they tend to be highly resistant to not continuing to be what they once were but are no longer.

Critical to this proneness is maintaining a sense of being an intergenerational family. And since the Pastoral Congregation is no longer a single cell family it will often resort to symbolic activity to maintain this illusion. One of the primary symbolic activities the Pastoral Congregation often employs is a token intergenerational moment at the beginning of its worship experience. This activity usually lasts ten or fifteen minutes at which time the children and youth exit to RE classes and the adults begin engaging their own worship experience.

When polls are taken to ascertain the effectiveness of this brief intergenerational moment, the children and youth will generally prefer to have their own age-friendly worship and it becomes apparent that it is mostly parents who are enamored of this symbolic activity. A more superficial part of this enamoredness is a show-and-tell quality but it basically roots in the parental desire to have a family orientation publicly dramatized.

In a Program Congregation this beginning intergenerational focus in the worship experience generally does four things. It lessens the time available to create a powerful worship experience for adults while divesting the children and youth of their own age-friendly opportunity. It bifurcates the focus of those present and normally requires a new beginning to elicit a spirit of adult worship. The language and perceptions used are, more often than not, over the head of most of the children participating. And it becomes a subtle use of children and youth to satisfy an adult need that could be addressed in some more spiritually satisfying manner.

In brief, it is usually a self-defeating activity that does little for children and youth and keeps adults from facing the realities of being a Program Congregation. Thus, it thwarts adults from creating intergenerational experiences that might truly satisfy their desire for a sense of family togetherness in worship. The question is: how can the need for a sense of intergenerational worship be created without resorting to symbolic tokenism?

One answer is to do away with this ineffective beginning moment in the "adult" worship service and create a series of intergenerational worship experiences that occupy the entire time of the service and focus on a theme that is spiritually profitable for all ages. This is not the same as dumbing down the worship experience. It requires, however, paying close attention to the use of time, language, and structure so that they engage all who are present. In brief, it is not just having another adult service with children and youth present. It is engaging the worship event as an extended family. And, it is creating an experience that attracts the attendance of adult families without children and youth and the older members of the congregation. It is far better to have a few real impactive intergenerational services scattered throughout the year than to burden every service with symbolic tokenism.

It is worth noting that many congregations are beginning to call intergenerational services "Extended Family Services" because such language implies that all ages are required for event success. Moreover, the term "extended family" implies a sense of unified community that the term "intergenerational" does not convey.

It should also be noted that the foregoing suggestion for the creation of significant Extended Family worship experiences will eventually reach a limit in both usefulness and facility capacity with the growth in attendance size in a Program Congregation. The larger a congregation grows the more difficult it is to create meaningful Extended Family worship experiences. And, eventually, the congregation may arrive at an attendance size that precludes all ages gathering in its sanctuary. Sooner or later, the Program Congregation may have to accept the requirement to cleanly separate its Sunday morning adult program from its children and youth program. There is no tragedy in this separation. It simply traffics on those dynamics that address issues of effectiveness and power in purpose.

Whatever the Program Congregation does about the need to create or delete intergenerational worship experiences, it can no longer afford to use the Family and Pastoral Congregation models as its guides. It must own up to the unique needs of its attendance size and address their realities if it is to be successful.

Two Worship Services or More

Often, congregations that are growing into Program size will also have space issues. Most Family Congregation and Pastoral Congregation facilities were built out of the limited growth vision of these respective mentalities devoid of more long-term views. The usual prognosis for dealing with such space issues is the establishment of two worship services and RE programs on Sunday morning. While this may be a temporary solution to attendance growth issues, it also poses subtle problems in completing the shift from a Pastoral to a Program Congregation.

Essentially, the problems rise from the division of the congregation into two different size worship services (usually one Pastoral and one Family) and RE programs while the rest of the ministry demands a program orientation. Those participating in one of these smaller attended services or programs tend to feel that they are in a Pastoral or Family Congregation and this feeling, in turn, tends to nurture both the desires and attitudes of this type congregation.

Consider seven ways these desires and attitudes are nurtured by the divided worship/RE experience. The first is that the division fosters an illusion about the real cellular nature of the congregation. The illusion is that the congregation is much smaller than in actuality. Moreover, one of these divided services is usually smaller than the other and, in all probability, will be more Family Congregation size than Pastoral Congregation size. But whatever the attendance size of the two services, two separate congregations are, indeed, being fostered in both spirit and perception that are smaller than the Program Congregation.

The second is that the two worship services and RE programs may actually be quite different in both content and spirit, having different impact and fostering a different sense of the nature of the experience for those attending. Some RE programs may occur only during one time frame and the choir may only sing at one of the services and the laity who participate may not be the same, bringing totally different words and spirits to the separate events. Even if the services are identically designed, the time of day, the number of participants, the spirit of the leadership, and the energy generated by all of these factors will converge into a different service. While such differences in service structure and spirit may not be important in Protestant congregations because of their peculiar perspectives, they do become important in non-Christian congregations.

Consequently, people who choose to consistently attend one service over the other may end up having a different experience and developing a different sense of the life of the congregation. Inevitably, this sense of the congregation will be that of an institution smaller than it actually is, with smaller needs. The difference between the sense of drama, power, and participation in one of two services (one averaging 100 in attendance and the other averaging 150 in attendance) compared to a single service averaging around 250 in attendance is consequential when it comes to actual dynamics and member perceptions.

The third spins out of this discrepancy in attendance dynamics. The sense of the congregation's need for monetary support tends to reflect the smaller vision framework of smaller attendance. Thus, this area of member stewardship also tends to affirm smaller need and support the spirit of scarcity that is characteristic of the smaller community. At a time when the congregation is actually in dire need of larger vision and a spirit of abundance in financial commitment, the smaller attendance at its divided worship experience speaks a contradictory message. The right hand of actuality says "stretch," and the left hand of illusion says "contract."

The fourth is that leadership must choose when it is best to have congregational meetings pertinent to its education and business when such is important to occur before or after a Sunday service. Inevitably, due to the logistics of time, this choice is after the second service. Those who have chosen to consistently attend the earlier service may gradually opt out of attending these meetings vital to understanding the ministry of the congregation. Thus, the character of commitment of the two services is often different and this contributes further to differing views of congregational life. Even if those who attend the earlier service choose to attend the second service when there is such a meeting, this decreases the attendance at the first service and changes its character. All of these choosing necessities may well destabilize the RE program since children and youth will normally attend when their parents attend.

The fifth is that, due to the smaller attendance of divided services, there is an encouragement to continue giving focus to Pastoral Congregation rituals and attitudes. One ritual example is the retention of Milestones/Joys and Concerns. One attitude example is the retention of the notion of being minister centered. All such retention contributes to slowing down the shift from a Pastoral to a Program Congregation.

The sixth is that people tend to join congregations that appeal to their sense of need. Thus, people who join as a result of attending the Pastoral Congregation size worship experience will join because this feels good to them. When the congregation is challenged to move on into more Program Congregation attitudes and ways of ministry, these people may both wonder about and question the validity of what is happening. Thus, the very success of membership growth created by going to two services may be subtly counterproductive to the ultimate goals of the shift to a Program Congregation.

The seventh is that people often have more personal reasons for desiring to use the two-service approach as a solution to space issues. There seems to be two such reasons that inevitably rise to the surface in congregational life during such considerations. One is the desire to remain in location because of a strong attachment to place over mission. Many Unitarian Universalists seem unable to distinguish between home as geography/building and home as community that rises from reason for being.

The other is that dividing the congregation's worship event produces smaller worship communities (Family and Pastoral attendance sizes) that enable congregants seriously attached to the characteristics of these smaller modes of community life to continue engaging them without the hassle of having to transist in either attitude or experience to Program Congregation mentalities. A debate over whether to remain in place by going to two services or move to a different, more growth-oriented location often hides these personal reasons under practical sounding rhetoric. Members with non-growth attitudes are remarkably clever about how they process their concerns.

All of the foregoing establishes another kind of catch-22 for the Program Congregation seeking legitimate ways for overcoming its space issues by going to two services. This is not to say that doing so is a bad move. It is only to say that the congregation needs to be aware of the negative possibilities inherent in doing so and address them as deliberately as possible and even put the two-service format on a time line. Nor are any of these stated dangers an argument for not going to two services. Such may be the only temporary solution to space issues. Or, it may be that circumstances conspire to make it impossible for the congregation to expand its ministry any other way than making two services a permanent way of doing worship.

It should be kept in mind that two worship experiences do, indeed, create several larger cells in which people can enter a sense of community belonging. And one of the basic characteristics of a Program Congregation is that it may, indeed, have two major worship experiences or more. Two things must be weighed in considering this factor. The first is the peculiarities of a Unitarian Universalist congregation when placed up beside a typical Protestant congregation and the resultant differences in community dynamic. The second traffics on this prior question, namely, is the goal simply to add cells for the sake of attendance growth or is the goal a bonded congregation that is profoundly devoted to the fulfillment of its religious mission.

All of the foregoing are cautions about not falling into the subtle traps that a two-service structure sets up. They are proposed as consciousness raising considerations so that the space issue is seen in light of the bigger picture of the shift from a Pastoral to a Program Congregation.

The foregoing also means at least three things for the congregation involved in this shift. It means that it cannot afford to allow the temporary divided worship experience to become a permanent solution to the issues of facilities space problems when other solutions are possible. It means that it must keep its consciousness high about the shift, be aware of the nuances that militate against completing the shift, and proceed with a deliberate game plan for making the shift happen. And, it also means that it must be deliberate about making its worship experience as consistent with being a Program Congregation as it is possible to do. Ultimately, this means it must seek to divest these services of all Pastoral Congregation modes and mentalities, irrespective of whether the divided services are temporary or permanent.

It must be kept in mind that for the congregation that has arrived at a Program Congregation attendance, whether it has two services or not, the worship experience will remain the only ministry touchstone for the majority of the members. The need for offering a multiplicity of alternative programmatic ways for entering the spirit of community remains just as high. And the necessity of bonding all the cells into a unified, mission-driven whole remains just as paramount. The challenge is to not allow the smaller mentalities produced by smaller attendance at divided services to create the illusion and foster the attitudes of being a Pastoral Congregation (or smaller) when the congregation, as a whole, is beyond the capacity to do effective ministry through such institutional visions.

Space

The human body is resiliently alive with the capacity to both reduce and enlarge its size. It can accommodate both experiences. This is not the case with inanimate creations such as buildings that are the homes of animate institutions. While the living institution can increase or decrease in size, the building that houses it can make no such accommodation without additional construction or destruction.

Consider an analogy. A congregation is like a mollusk that can grow no larger than its shell home grows. This is one of the primary principles that govern congregational growth, namely, that available space will determine the extent of attendance growth.

But, unlike the mollusk that can grow and fill the available crevices of its shell home, congregational space sends out messages of growth limitation. For example, a room of a certain size sends out a message that only so many children of a certain age can be happy within its confines. To put this differently, space environments are governed by how much square footage is needed per child at any given age in order to be accommodating to an effective educational experience.

A sanctuary will send out a similar message to newcomers. If it is 80% full its message will be that there is insufficient space for the newcomer to continue attending. So even an inanimate creation such as a building has an animate psychology about how its space gets filled with people. Of course, if the drama of what is happening in that space is compelling enough, people will ignore the space message for a while. But even compelling-ness cannot overcome a sustained message of no vacancy.

Thus, it makes no difference how dynamic a Program Congregation might be in its ministry; if it does not have the physical space by which to accommodate growth it will plateau in attendance. What this means is that the vital Program Congregation will inevitably be experiencing space problems and will continue to do so even if it is in the process of building more space. A building program that does not end is one of the most dramatic signs that a Program Congregation is fulfilling its mission.

When the vital Program Congregation runs out of space it only has one of three major options. It can expand its facilities on the property upon which it presently resides, if such is possible. It can move to a larger property environment and build more accommodating facilities so that it can continue to grow. Or, it can make room internally for further growth by sending out a segment of its membership to start a new congregation in a different geographic location. If it does none of these it will simply languish in a non-growth plateau zone that is sustained by some form of revolving-door membership or it will begin a membership decline. Even if it decides to stay at its present location without expanding its space but accommodating to its growth potential by going to a two-service structure, if its attendance grows it will eventually arrive back at the same non-growth plateau where it started.

An interesting phenomenon in our religious movement is the simultaneous and contradictory love affair we have with smallness and the desire to be socially transforming. It rarely occurs to us that the space problem solutions we are most prone to favor generally militate against our deep desire to be socially transforming. When we look around us it is obvious that the institutions that impact society are large enough to have the resources to draw attention to their values. An example is the ability to project the congregation's values via media into the social environment or the capacity to have programs that attract total community-wide attention. Yet, we seem to prefer a practice of constant cellular division and small land purchases that make such growth into largeness and its potential consequential impact impossible.

Thus, in actual practice, the obvious message of our religious movement's behavior is that we would prefer to have small sized institutions in which to feel comfortable than to impact the world around us. Ineffective social action projects that only address symptoms and politically correct posturing seem to be ways we believe will compensate for the lack of the power of largeness. But history suggests that such is an illusion. When was the last time you heard of a Unitarian Universalist congregation under the attendance size of a Resource Congregation that boasted a story about external community social transformation? Small may be beautiful but it can also be impotent. It behooves us to include in our discussions about space problem solutions this more expansive dimension of the power to transform the social order. In other words, when considering the solution to space issues we might wish to ask what solution will maximize our capacity to be a transforming agent in the world. Attendance size capacity becomes a major issue in seeking to answer this question.

Space, then, is an issue around which visionary dialogue constantly takes place within the leadership of the vital mission-oriented Program Congregation. The principle governing this is that if a congregation is fulfilling its mission it cannot stop growing in attendance unless there is some natural environmental prohibition.

The Two Church Syndrome

Once a congregation reaches a Pastoral size in attendance there is a tendency for many who are attracted to the Religious Education program to give that aspect of ministry their fullest attention to the exclusion of the rest of the congregation's ministry. This shrinking of the size of the congregation through pared-down focus and commitment could be the result of any number of parental or member desires. For example, their only concern about the congregation's existence might be that it makes possible for their children to be exposed to liberal values not available in the secular environment. Or, they may wish their children to have the religious liberal ammunition to respond to the conservative religious language and concepts they are normally exposed to by classmates in the public school system. Or, it could be a way, through narrowed focus, of actually paring down the congregation's size in order to retain a sense of family or community that gets lost to attendance growth. On the other hand, they may be so enamored of and inspired by religious education for children and youth that they much prefer this participation on Sunday mornings to that of adult worship. Whatever the reason, the tendency of the paring of focus is to further exacerbate the issues of the Pastoral Congregation to Program Congregation transition. The end result is the possible creation of what is often euphemistically called "the upstairs and downstairs churches."

This is a division of membership commitment into what appears to be exclusive areas of the congregation's ministry on Sunday mornings. One division is a commitment to children and youth religious education. The other is a commitment to the adult programming and worship experience. Unfortunately, many of those who participate in this divisive focus tend to allow it to spill over into their total view of commitment. Thus, those who focus on the RE ministry (the downstairs church) often have no inkling of what is happening in the rest of the congregation's ministry and do not participate in other aspects of the congregation's life. And those whose only concern on Sunday mornings is the adult worship experience (the upstairs church) build their own exclusive view as to what facets of the congregation's ministry are important and remain uninformed as to the learning experience of those children and youth who might constitute the congregation's future.

Since the Program Congregation already faces critical issues that have to do with the creation of common visions and over-coming its nemesis of unbonded and isolated cells, this larger division compounds its problems and dramatizes a larger fractured view of the nature of its ministry. In brief, permitting the upstairs and downstairs division to thrive, let alone exist, threatens its spiritual well-being and moves it further toward becoming nothing more than an institutional umbrella for a variety of smaller and separate congregations. This is tantamount to a loss of all of the benefits that are offered by making the shift to a Program Congregation.

Depending on its membership makeup and its internal dynamics, congregations that face this issue must figure out how it is best addressed. However, there are some things that most every congregation can do to lessen the grip this division of commitment might have on its life. Here are a few:

+ It can make sure that the mission statement of any facet of its ministry resides under the congregation's overall religious mission statement. It can ask its leaders to periodically have both read in unison at the beginning of meetings and to reflect on the implications of how these statements work to mutual benefit.

+ It can ask the Nominating Committee (or whatever bodies choose workers), with the willing participation of its staff and ministers, to constantly move leadership around into different facets of ministry for cross-fertilization and the building of commitment to the whole.

+ It can create meaningful extended worship experiences that symbolize its wholeness and it can incorporate some of the rituals children and youth use in their age-friendly worship services and vice versa.

+ It can create other extended family experiences that allow all ages to benefit from each other's human struggles and life views.

+ It can establish policies that do not permit members to volunteer for Sunday morning RE ministries more than half of a teaching year or more than one year without a break, with a strong encouragement for these members to experience the adult worship service so they can bring the insights back into their next teaching experience. And, in reverse, it can create a policy that requires prior commitment to the Sunday morning adult worship experience or other adult spiritual growth experiences before a member is encouraged to assume a teaching position.

To put this differently, policies can be established that guide the selection of teachers from a pool of members who have demonstrated a commitment to the congregation's total ministry beyond religious education or the adult worship experience themselves. This may be one of the more critical aspects of dealing with the nurturance of the upstairs and downstairs syndrome.

It seems apparent that this divisionistic commitment is seriously encouraged by the recruitment of workers to the Sunday morning RE program who have no solid grounding in perspectives about either the total ministry of the congregation or the fundamental beliefs of the Unitarian Universalist religious experience. In a zeal to enlist support for this vital ministry this grounding is often overlooked without understanding that it does a disservice to the individual volunteer, the RE pupil, and the ministry of the whole congregation. And, it becomes an unwitting support of the division into two distinctive congregations.

If a Committee On Ministry exists it must do its job of holding high the mission of the congregation and the notion that ministry is everything the congregation does to fulfill this mission. It must directly and deliberately involve itself in analyzing why the division exists and make recommendations relative to its solution. It must be insistent and follow up on its recommendations. It must not permit the division to persist because such a persistence would be harmful to the congregation's ministry and spiritual well-being and one of the COM's primary responsibilities is diminishing such harm and increasing such well-being. It should be the primary mover in addressing any and all divisions that have an adverse effect on the congregation's ministry.

The staff and professional ministers must be on the same page about recognizing and addressing the issues inherent in this division. They must be willing to support policies that diminish the existence of this division. They must constantly be aware of not falling into well-meaning activities that lend it support. They must constantly be discussing how to cause the division to disappear. They must cooperate rather than compete when it comes to enlisting volunteers. For these basic leaders to impact this issue, they must have a common commitment to the congregation's mission over the supporting purpose of their own particular ministry responsibilities. They must endorse the notion that the part exists for the sake of the whole.

Whatever a congregation does to address this issue when its existence becomes apparent, it is obvious that the primary solution lies in prevention. Prevention is a deliberate program that orients members into a holistic view of the congregation's ministry and a refusal to permit members who do not participate in such a view to shape the Sunday morning experience, whatever it might be. If this issue is not adequately addressed the end result will be a significant lessening of the potential synergistic power of the Program Congregation.

Goaling

,   Goaling is normally called "long-range planning." Goaling is used here as a way of emphasizing the targeting nature of the planning process. But, by whatever name, its function is to look beyond the present and into the future in terms of need, wish, and mission.

The goals of the Pastoral Congregation tend to be inward oriented. This is both its strength and weakness. Its strength is that it embraces and celebrates its own being as religious community. It provides spiritual arms for mutual affirmation and support. This affirming and supporting charge the community environment with warmth and caring. And all of this strokes the worth of its individual members in a manner of realness beyond the artificiality of the culture.

Its weakness is the very inwardness of this orientation. So strong is the devotion to community that, once arriving at the fullness of its attendance-size capacities, it may find subtle ways of shutting down its welcoming spirit as a means of protecting this community from dilution. And it may convert its sense of mission to that of social action as a way of subverting negative feelings about this shutdown. Social action can be a form of evangelism that tends not to threaten the congregation with an influx of new members while, at the same time, creating a sense of investment nobility and mission fulfillment.

Normally, if the Pastoral Congregation has long-range goals these are maintenance oriented and have to do with such internalized foci as facilities improvement, ways to enhance its sense of community or upgrade its religious education program, or pastoral care delivery.

On the other hand, if it has arrived at its attendance plateau level, it may be looking at a variety of ways to break through this stalemate. If that is the case, then, its goaling process must be a wrestling with how to overcome the stasis of this plateau. Without translating this wrestling into a Long Range Plan it will simply languish in the mediocrity of this stasis.

The Program Congregation has a different strength and weakness in respect to goaling. Its strength is its ability to provoke spiritual growth through its programs and to transform socially through the resources of its attendance size. Its weakness is its tendency to fragment into isolated groups of individual interest that come to exist for the sake of themselves. Thus, the very strength of its program character is easily converted into becoming nothing more than a support for that fracturing form of individualism that is the enemy of a unifying mission and the transforming power of commonality. And, like the Pastoral Congregation, when succumbing to this fragmentation, may convert its religious mission into a social action orientation that basks in the nobility of transforming visions with little corresponding realization.

Thus, the Program Congregation has a profound need for a spirited process of Long Range Planning that enables it to keep its programs bonded to its religious mission and empowers its transforming capacities. This planning must provide

+ a clear vision of its potential future
+ a mission motivation for its members
+ a glue for bonding its disparate parts
+ a way of elevating the quality of its ministry
+ a means of measuring incremental accomplishment

This plan needs to be hammered out and owned by its lay leadership, its staff and ministers and adopted by the whole congregation. It must be diligently promoted throughout the congregation's life and become a part of every agent of its ministry. It is this plan that will keep it mission oriented and become its visionary heartbeat and one of the sources of its membership attraction.

But to do so it must have certain tensional qualities. It must stretch the imagination while being attainable. It must inspire while being grounded. It must transcend the individual while bonding individuals. It must promise a new future while remaining anchored in the present.

Without this kind of well-developed and carefully implemented Long Range Plan the Program Congregation will languish in the bondage of inertia. It is simply too large in attendance size to move toward a different future without this form of deliberateness. This is one of the primary reasons why the capacities of visionary and skilled leadership are so critical to its existence. Only with such leadership comes this kind of deliberateness.

Scarcity and Abundance

The Program Congregation will never cease needing more financial resources to expand its program and staff and to create change in the world around it. This is the given of its mission and ministry state of being.

This continuing need can be addressed in two primary ways. First, it can be approached from the spirit of scarcity. This is the view that its members are hard-pressed financially and that the congregation is probably doing as well as it can. This view normally calls for the attitude of justification, the notion that whatever increase in the budget is asked for during the annual canvass campaign must be accompanied by a corresponding detailed substantiation. The perspective is that increases must be proven worthy of member consideration since they are already giving so generously.

This spirit of scarcity promotes two philosophies toward member giving. One philosophy is that any vision for the future must be tailored to the scarcity of resources. The other is that, whatever the vision, people must not be asked to stretch their financial commitment too far. Combined, these two philosophies generally harvest precisely what they are designed to harvest, namely, low motivation and low results. The larger end result of this low result is that the Program Congregation tied to the scarcity approach will always operate financially in a maintenance mode. This mode, in turn, generates further low vision, low motivation, low commitment, and low accomplishment. It reproduces itself. And those who live in this mode long enough convert it into a self-satisfied lifestyle.

It is arriving at this place of self-satisfaction that causes both attendance and membership to plateau. A Program

Congregation can live minimally on this plateau for years and never go any place it has never been before. And many Program Congregations have developed this lifestyle as their comfort zone.

The other option for addressing the Program Congregation's continuing need for resources is to approach the issue from the spirit of abundance. This view is that its members have ample financial resources and that the congregation can do far better than it has up to this point in time. This normally calls for an attitude of possibility; the notion that whatever increase in the budget is asked for during the annual canvass campaign can easily be attained if the members are sufficiently motivated.

The approach of abundance usually promotes its own two philosophies. One philosophy is that the congregation's vision of the future should be expanded to match its untapped possibilities. The other is that people should be asked to stretch their financial commitment as far as they can to accomplish this vision. Combined, these philosophies tend to harvest precisely what they are designed to harvest, namely, high motivation and high result. The end result of this larger result is that the Program Congregation tied to the abundance approach will always operate financially in a growth mode. This mode, in turn, generates further high vision, high motivation, high commitment, and high accomplishment. And those who live in this mode long enough convert it into a self-challenging lifestyle.

It is arriving at this place that causes both attendance and membership to expand. A Program Congregation can live maximally in this challenge and continue to go places it has never been before. And, again, this is because the issue is not available resources. The spirit of abundance will normally glean twice as much from the same available resource as the spirit of scarcity. The heart is the user and the spirits of scarcity and abundance are statements of the heart's preference. The heart will make happen whatever it wishes to happen, with whatever is available. In brief, the spirit of scarcity always sees what is not possible while the spirit of abundance always sees what is possible. It is not just an attitude toward resources; it is an attitude toward life.

The question is: "Given the choice between an uninspiring mode of maintenance or an inspiring mode of challenge, into which kind of congregation would I prefer to invest my life and resources?"

Most people would choose the latter because they wish their life investments to connect with excitement, nobility, and a better future.

But even if a congregation chooses to approach its future in the spirit of abundance, there is an additional problem it must overcome in order for this approach to be successful. In our religious movement, even the leadership that espouses high vision will often recommend low means for accomplishing this vision. That is, their vision will be geared to the spirit of abundance while their means of accomplishment will be geared to the spirit of scarcity.

This ambivalent leadership is sometimes expressed through a cautionary approach to raising the challenge of the giving guide. This cautionary spirit will advise a "go slow" policy. An example is increasing the level of the giving guide a little at a time so as not to cause people to feel guilty if they cannot match the recommended percentages. While we encourage both ourselves and the world around us to feel supremely guilty about being unresponsive to social need outside of congregational life, we will claim that being made to feel guilty about miserly giving is a violation of a guiltless theology. We seem far more frightened of feeling guilty about a failure of financial commitment than we are about being institutionally and socially impotent. To say that this yoking of abundance and scarcity is counterproductive would be a gross understatement. It is like yoking a giant and a dwarf as if the dwarf were equal to the challenge of the giant.

This low means of accomplishment has two parts. It asks far too little of a religious group that normally lives in the upper half of national income levels. This minimal asking is reflected in Fair Share Giving Guides that range on the lower end from one-half of a percent to a range on the upper end of 3 or, maybe, 4 percent of gross annual income. The other part of this low means of accomplishment is normally an articulation of apologetic loopholes by which members can escape this minimal giving guide, thus, obviating even this ho-hum non-challenge.

The Program Congregation that wishes to achieve a challenge mode of abundance and sustain this exciting posture of existence will need to escape this oxymoronic style of leadership. And the only way it can effectively do so is to make its Fair Share Giving Guide a reflection of its spirit of abundance. This means at least two things. One is raising the percentage levels to a range on the lower end to at least around 1 and 2 percent to a range on the upper end to between 8 and 10 percent. Another is approaching this giving level in an unapologetic manner that offers no loopholes, expects its members' mission-oriented commitment to make the right decision, and understands that those who cannot make this leap will make their own decision with clear conscience without seeking further justification. After all, that which is at stake here is far more than an internal ministry that offers possible transformation to its members. It is an external ministry that offers possible transformation to the society in which it exists.

To say this another way, the Program Congregation that wishes to live an existence that generously partakes of its grand possibilities must be unapologetic for its vision of nobility and for a giving guide that traffics on this nobility. The will to approach mission and ministry in this fashion will be easily detected in the growth, excitement, and influence of its entire institutional presence.

Of course there will be those who will challenge this approach to mission fulfillment. And one of the common notions put forth as support of such challenges is that Unitarian Universalists generously give to other causes aside from their congregation. This of course is spurious reasoning. It ignores the obvious fact that conservative religionists not only strive for a 10% contribution to their congregation but also support the multiplicity of conservative causes in the social order, thus normally giving far more than this 10%. Otherwise, who is it that sustains the conservative enterprises in the cultural environment?

Another common argument that seeks to downgrade the high level of conservative giving while justifying the low level of liberal giving is espousing the notion that liberals give out of their desire to see good things happen while conservatives give out of guilt and an attempt to buy fire-insurance from hell. Anyone who has experienced any time in religious conservative movements know that this is liberal nonsense. Conservative religionists do not give for either of these reasons. They give because they are committed to the notion that they have a message that the world must have for its redemption. If liberals believed as strongly about their own message their level of giving would be competitive with that of conservatives.

Congregations that wish to impact the world with their liberal values must positively meet the challenge of the high level of conservative commitment rather than forever seeking to justify their own low level of commitment.

Distinct Religious Identity

All of the foregoing nuances of transition combine into what is critical to the Program Congregation's success, namely, a distinct religious identity. It is this identity that announces its self-image and its role in the larger community and informs that larger community of its goals and power to make these goals a reality. In brief, the congregation's social influence is bound up in this identity. If that identity is blurred or negative, so is this influence. If it is clear and positive, so is this influence.

This means that the identity cannot be simply left to unplanned chance as to how its components might come together. It must be deliberately created if the social image it projects is to be what it wishes. This means that the shift to a Program Congregation must be seen holistically and an overall plan designed to effect the transition in a manner of minimum energy expended and maximum power created. Drifting into the transition becomes maximum energy expended and minimum power created. It portents a languishing mission and ministry.

Normally, the identities of our individual congregations are based on a conglomerate of ministry perspectives in the same way that our typical mission statements are a conglomerate of ministry facets. They will imbibe of such perspectives as: "We are that congregation that has a wonderful community spirit." "We are a congregation so skilled in how we do things that we are superior to other UU congregations." "We are a congregation that invests a great deal of energy and resources in social action." "We are a congregation that gives a strong focus to the family and our RE program reflects this strength." Such statements of identity tend to ignore the congregation's religious mission and the message of transformation it might have to offer to both individuals and society. Rather, they are statements of pride about facets of ministry focus.

For congregations trapped in this ministry facet mentality, there is a useful alternative way of approaching the issue of identity. It is by asking two questions about the congregation's existence. The first is: "What is its business in the world?" This is the question about mission. The second is: "How will it accomplish this business?" This is the question about ministry. Mission is why the congregation exists and ministry is everything it does to make that mission a reality. It is the difference between motive and means, between purpose and fulfillment. Without a perceptive understanding of this distinction, a congregation will forever confuse why it exists with how it makes this why a reality. And its social identity will reflect this confusion.

Conclusion

What the foregoing examples show is that when the shift is being made from a Pastoral Congregation to a Program Congregation, all of the systemic forms and processes must be made to harmonize to avoid bleeding off the very energy that is required for effective ministry.

Any profound growth experience requires bringing all parts into harmony with that which is at the heart of the growth. The shift from being a Pastoral Congregation to being a Program Congregation is a profound growth experience. Wherever a congregation might be in completing this shift, it will be an act of wisdom to look at its processes and organization in a holistic manner and engage whatever does not fit or whatever seems to retard the completion.

This will require an up-front acknowledgment of what is being lost in the shift as well as what is being gained. These losses and gains should not only be recognized for what they are, they should be released and grasped in some ritualistic manner of movement from past into present, thus, opening the future to creative shaping. Without such recognition and rituals, much energy and time will be wasted fighting needless battles of resistance on various fronts of congregational life.

It is best to awaken to a new day and engage it with full awareness than drowse into a new day and engage it with partial awareness. Better to complete a task as quickly as possible so its fruits can be enjoyed as soon as possible than completing it slowly and only enjoying its fruits a little at a time. Awakening fully is not synonymous with hurriedness. It is synonymous with awareness and deliberateness. It is a synonym for being energized and alive.

13

Perceptual Shifts

The shift from a Pastoral Congregation to a Program Congregation is attended by certain perceptual shifts. While some members may never be able to make these shifts because of preference or psychological need, the leadership and larger majority of the congregation must make them if completion is to be attained. Following are a few of these perceptual shifts. Again it is important to keep in mind that the lists are not mutually exclusive. Some may exist in either. They represent primary tendencies that derive from the dynamics of attendance-size cultures and the possibilities that such cultures are prone to engender. Thus, they are descriptive caricatures rather than social judgments.

Pastoral	Program
Whole for the part	Part for the whole
Personal fulfillment	Personal growth
Community as goal	Community as consequence
Maintenance	Movement
Small is beautiful	Big is powerful
Affirming	Challenging

Pastoral	Program
Intimacy focus	Transformation focus
For the sake of ourselves	For the sake of the world

It is obvious, as Theodore W. Johnson points out, that this shift is one of changing the culture of the congregation. In this respect, culture is an integrated pattern of attitudes, actions, and celebrations that reflect a set of beliefs and institutional attendance-size dynamics. Thus, a change in culture necessitates, as its prerequisite, a major alteration of ways of seeing. This means the shift is both profound and revolutionary in the best sense of these terms. It is profound in that it requires a new way of seeing the mission and ministry of the congregation. It is revolutionary in that this new way of seeing calls for radically different ways of approaching the fulfillment of this mission and ministry.

14

Success Review

I perceive there to be five major areas that impact the success of the Program Congregation's ministry in a critical fashion.

Two of these areas are pervasive and diffused in the congregation's ministry. One is the manner of board governance and how this governance impacts multiple concerns such as agent empowerment, decision making, focus of energy, and mutual trust. The need to move toward some form of policy governance as a way of positively enhancing such concerns seems imperative for maximum success in the Program-size congregation. The values of this type of governance have already been underscored several places in prior chapters. It is simply important to emphasize this need as critical to success.

The other area is professional and lay leadership adequate to the demands of the Program Congregation's complex ministry. Since the usual ministry energy demands are high and the usual available member energy to meet these demands is low, sufficient Called and paid leadership becomes critical. Moreover, the quality and stability of the lay leadership required cannot be left to either chance or a "warm body" approach to fulfillment. I suggest that an effective Program Congregation will have a minimum of two professional ministers. In addition, there will be a multiplicity of full- and part-time staff people. These people will represent ministries such as administration-communication, volunteer coordination, religious faith development (lifespan), membership, counseling, music, custodial care, youth, young adults, finances, child care, facilities maintenance, etc.

The third and fourth of these major areas are distinctive and highly visible and serve as the primary entry points for people into the congregation's ministry. One is the Sunday morning event that consists of the children and youth worship and educational program and the adult worship experience. Since this event will be the only constant touchstone for the majority of the congregation's membership with its ministry, its quality and drama is indispensable to success. It must do two things effectively. It must motivate toward commitment and it must create a desire for further spiritual growth. It is this commitment that will provide the resources necessary to sustain the congregation's ministry. It is this desire that will move people into sustained programmatic growth experiences.

This created desire emphasizes the fourth of these major areas, namely, a deliberately designed and powerful adult spiritual faith development program. The deliberate design is a preconceived range of program needs that moves its participants toward spiritual wholeness. The power comes from a careful instituting of this design in a reoccurring and time-cycling manner. Such a program must be broad in that it covers a wide variety of program themes and duration so that there is something of attraction that suits the need and schedule of every member. It must be deep in that it ranges from a beginning level of religious exploration to an advanced level of religious exploration. Such a program requires both professional and lay leadership who have a "can see" vision of long-term programming need and a "can do" commitment that makes it all a dynamic reality. In brief, the adult program must be a mini-seminary in configuration, content, and coverage. Nothing less will satisfy the demand of this programming need.

To say it another way, this is not a program designed from a "who would like to give a program or lead a workshop?" approach. This is an approach that knows what it wants and refuses to be sabotaged by laissez-faire methods of construction. Only a perceptive depth of need, an expansive vision of fulfillment, and a deliberate plan of execution will make this kind of profound program happen.

The fifth area partakes of both pervasiveness and diffusedness and, likewise, distinctiveness and visibility. It is an organization that is deliberately designed to deliver ministry in a manner consistent with the size dynamics and the program thrust of the Program Congregation. Again, if the Program Congregation is still organized as a Pastoral Congregation it is organized for failure. In making this transition the leadership should examine every facet of institutional organization and not just jerry-rig. That is, it should create a whole new structural way of looking at ministry delivery, both internally and externally (inclusive of social action, advertising, and proclaiming its message to the larger community). Impact requires delivery before it can be impact.

Any congregation wishing to either engage or complete the Pastoral to Program shift should give careful consideration to these five major areas of impact.

15

Cultural Indicators

As a final review it might be useful to look at the Pastoral and Program Congregations in profile of those factors that indicate their respective institutional cultures.

The Pastoral Congregation

Size of Total Attendance

The dynamics are governed by a total attendance of between 76 and 175 people.

Manner of Membership Relating

The membership relates as a large single-cell body. Most of the people who attend know or recognize each other as family units and tend to know the names of family members. The quality is that of being part of a large extended family.

Style of Basic Leadership

The basic leader is the minister who engages members as friends, cares for their pastoral needs, provides their basic growth experiences, and serves as their spiritual sage. While the laity provides multiple leadership roles they normally do so under the trusting guidance of the minister.

Nature of Manifested Community

A prideful sense of mutually embracing and mutually affirming community bonds the membership in unity. When this membership gathers at major events it does so to celebrate its own being as community. This sense of community normally finds a strong internal focus and is usually viewed as critical to the institution's identity.

Structure of Reflecting Organization

Aside from the minister as focal leader, the Pastoral Congregation will normally be board driven in respect to organization. This board's constituency will tend to combine leadership that represents major facets of the congregation's ministry, inclusive of financial and program ministries. The structures it designs will all impinge on facilitating the sense of community.

Locus of Decision Making

Beyond the minister and the board, there will be a pervasive sense of democratic ownership of decision-making processes by the general membership. The spirit of these processes will be directed toward inclusive consensus. The congregation, when it meets as a whole to engage decision making, will wish to invest in a mode of micromanagement that is consistent with its sense of democratic ownership.

The Program Congregation

Size of Total Attendance

The dynamics are governed by an attendance of between 176 and around 700.

Manner of Membership Relating

The congregation will be made up of multiple cells of varied numerical sizes. Its members will relate more like being part of a small prescribed village where they will only actually know a limited number of people out of a much larger whole. Yet, they will have an institutional identity and sense of relating that absorbs more people than can be known. They will have a tendency to develop this sense of identity by connecting their small-cell relatings to their large-cell relatings.

Style of Basic Leadership

There will be several ministerial leaders or a team of ministerial co-leaders who will supervise a staff of full- and part-time leaders. There will be an essential spirit of partnership between ministerial, staff and lay leadership and a collaborative team approach that will bond the whole of these leaders in common vision and direction. This spirit will be that of Shared Ministry. The ministerial leadership will be viewed as mentor and their function will be to create teamness of spirit.

Nature of Manifested Community

Whatever sense of community exists will be determined by three factors. One factor will be geared to the nature of the congregation's programmatic ministry, inclusive of its Sunday drama. A second factor will be geared to the capacity of the key ministerial and lay leadership to instill in the membership a sense of common mission. The third factor will be geared to the clarity and inspirational quality of its stated religious mission and the extent to which this statement is used to guide the total community life. Whatever this sense of community, if successful, it will be diffused and connected to overarching ideals of nobility.

Structure of Reflecting Organization

Its various facets of ministry will be divided and organized into kinship focus, empowered with authority to function effectively, and given guidance by mission-oriented policies. Through this process of collaborative ministry division, the board moves beyond the limitations of micromanagement to providing basic spiritual and visionary leadership. The structure of these divisions will be creative rather than uniform amongst Program Congregations, constructed according to vision and need.

Locus of Decision Making

Decision-making authorities will be spread out among the various entities of ministry. Such spreading will be geared to the need for smaller groups making decisions and rapid processing of decision making as a way of responding to the size dynamics of the congregation life. The end result, if done effectively, will be that of pervasive shared power.

16

Making the Shift a Reality

Moving Beyond Resistance

Even if a congregant becomes fully aware of the difference between the Pastoral and Program Congregations and
understands the rewards offered by the Program Congregation,
she/he may still not be willing to make a shift in allegiance.
People tend to join congregations that appeal to their personal
needs and visions. And people who join Pastoral Congregations
normally do so because of the appeal to community.

Those with the greatest personal need for such community
involvement may see the shift to the Program Congregation
lifestyle as a profound threat to the loss of community. This
threat is emotional in nature and cannot be adequately addressed
by appeals to logic. There must be a similar emotional appeal
that rises from persuasive conviction. There must also be some
genuine assurance that the issue of community retention will be
adequately addressed before they are willing to lend support to
this shift. And those with the most profound need for the social
support of community may not be willing to even consider this
shift. They may see the loss as too great. Even though these
members may represent a very small minority in congregational
life, their resistance will constitute a concern for those who see

the grander possibilities of the shift.

The bottom line is that the congregation that knows it is in the best interest of its mission and ministry to deliberately make this shift will only do so when it accepts the fact that everyone will not get on board. This acceptance, within itself, is a part of making the shift for it implies a movement from the notion that making everybody happy within the community ("leave no person behind") is what the congregation is all about to the notion that challenging human transformation is what the congregation is all about.

Total Honesty

As the congregation's leadership grasps what is involved in either initiating or completing this shift, total honesty about what is involved is necessary for people to take ownership and exhibit those attitudes that will ensure success. Thus, whatever will be the losses characterized by moving from a Pastoral Congregation posture should be named. And whatever will be the gains characterized by moving into a Program Congregation posture should be named. People need this total picture of losses and gains so the decision to support the shift is grounded in the realities it represents. They also need to know how the leadership anticipates dealing with other issues of the shift such as the nurturing of community, decision making, and the organizing of the institution.

People who have a full picture of the meaning of the shift are more likely to be both supportive and motivated to invest energy in making it happen.

17

Type and Preference

People tend to join religious institutions because they perceive that certain important needs will be meet. The Family, Pastoral, Program, and Resource Congregations all have something different to offer when it comes to human need fulfillment.

The Ground of Attraction

What is it that attracts members to any given congregation? The answer to that question lies in an axiom that tends to govern human experience, namely, that similar kinds are mutually attracted. This is expressed in the familiar adage "Birds of a feather flock together." And while opposites may attract there must be a sufficient amount of commonality for this form of attraction, given time, to stave off being repelled. It remains that commonality is the essential agent of bonding in human experience. This is so even when the bonding is of strange bedfellows.

The Ground of Deciding

Joining a congregation is, at its heart, an emotion-based decision. The rational decisions that people give for being attracted to a given congregation, if pushed backwards, will find an emotional root. Likewise, rational descriptions of what people are looking for in a religious context are descriptions of emotional preference. Such decisions and descriptions are grounded in those felt needs that anchor in the deepest part of one's self and are reflective of a peculiar cultural background.

That one person wants one form of community and another person wants a different form of community has to do with an emotional makeup that reflects differing views of personal need and differing levels of personal fulfillment. That one person is turned on by a certain architectural and aesthetical environment and certain religious rituals and another person is turned on by the opposite is sourced in each person's cultural past and may have no reasonable explanation for the present except that they are part of the stored experience impressions and visual imageries that converge to make up the individual's unique way of engaging the world.

What all this means is that the notion that any given Unitarian Universalist Congregation can appeal to everyone is spurious thinking. Such thinking leads to spurious conclusions about what constitutes congregational failure to entice people into membership that, in turn, produces spurious guilt and spurious activities. Each congregation has its own unique culture and that culture may have no attraction whatsoever to people raised in a culture of differing uniqueness.

This is one reason why races and classes are so difficult to blend. To be welcoming of all races, for example, may be the rightful posture of a Unitarian Universalist congregation, but to expect that people of all racial backgrounds will find a common attraction to the congregation's lifestyle is a view that does not understand the nuances and needs of cultural differences. That is, different cultures exist because they are different and the very makeup of these differences dictates different grounding of emotional attraction. For example, an African-American who is broadly liberal in respect to social and political issues may still prefer an emotion-based style of religious worship typical of many black congregations of the Deep South. Being socially and politically liberal and being attracted to current classical Unitarian Universalist worship styles are not synonymous.

Thus, liberals carry around a lot of self-imposed guilt based on the spurious notion that a congregation, because it has a rational focus and a liberal theology, ipso facto should be appealing to anyone of any cultural background who also might be a rational liberal. This illusion obviates the very notion that cultural differences produce a complex of unique emotional preferences. Normally, those people of different races attracted to liberal white congregations are thusly attracted because of similarities of cultural background and not because liberal white worship and programs constitute a cultural melting-pot experience.

A wise congregation will, therefore, forget about trying to be all things to all people and concentrate on being what the community in which it exists needs. After all, this is what sharing the good news is all about: couching that good news in those words and all those cultural mannerisms necessary to the understanding and appeal of the listener. Any congregation that cannot position itself in its community of existence in this manner will fail and, at best, persist in stagnation. If successful, a congregation will reflect the constituency of its social environment to the degree of its own emotional appeal to this constituency.

Spiritual Environment

Every congregation has a spiritual environment that is at the heart of its attraction to newcomers. Basic to this environment is the essential culture of its ministry as defined by its attendance-size type: Family, Pastoral, Program, or Resource.

If there is a congruency in how each type is being processed then all is well in respect to attracting the membership of newcomers because the newcomer is joining a reality that speaks to harmony. However, it is possible that the reality the newcomer encounters is that of disharmony.

Due to either desire or unawareness, the congregation may be conflicted because it is one type based on attendance size and a different type based on actual function. For example, a congregation may be a Program Congregation in respect to attendance while, in reality, functioning like a Pastoral Congregation. If there is a pattern as to why people join its membership then this is a clue as to where its energies find dominant expression. And the tendency in this domination will be for its functional type to take precedent over its attendance type.

If it is conflicted in this manner, then its ministry will be characterized by energy investments that pull in different directions and obviate effectiveness. In turn, the messages of its spiritual environment will also be conflicted for newcomers. For example, the message of functioning like a Pastoral Congregation may be that of a welcoming and embracing community while the largeness of the Program Congregation's attendance size may belie this message. The end result may be either a lack of positive response on the part of newcomers or an act of joining grounded in misperceived reality. In either case, the congregation's ministry stands in jeopardy of being affected negatively.

But there are other factors that make up a congregation's spiritual environment besides the characteristics of its attendance type. There is a message that is presented very graphically to newcomers that issues from the congregation's physical space. Even if the congregation feels right to the newcomer, there may not be ample physical space for that person's inclusion in membership. If the sanctuary is full because something exciting is happening, this very fullness may send a message to the newcomer that there is no more room for inclusion in this excitement. For example, a Pastoral Congregation that has reached the limits of its physical space in terms of attendance may choose neither to establish two services to open up more space nor to expand its facilities out of fear of losing its community charm. In either case the decision is tantamount to hanging out a "No Vacancy" sign.

There is also a message that is presented to newcomers about space that is less tangible than physical space but just as felt and just as real. Some church consultants call it psychological space. There might be ample physical space while the attitude and spirit of the congregation's members indicate that the door to membership is closed. For example, a Pastoral Congregation may have plenty of physical space while pushing the limits of its size. Sensing that it may lose its feeling of community if it grows any more it may, by unofficial agreement, verbalize openness because that is the theologically correct thing to do while, concurrently, sending newcomers a psychological message that they are welcome to visit but not join. The message is: "Go away a little closer."

While the foregoing represent negative illustrations about the resistance to making natural transitions from one attendance type to another, here is a positive illustration of deliberateness about completing a transition that would send out messages of space welcome. One of our congregations had languished in membership growth for years because its views and organization were geared to that of a Pastoral Congregation while its attendance size was far into that of a Program Congregation and newcomers could not get a clear message about the nature of its real being. But it suddenly awakened to its need to complete the transition to a Program Congregation and to the fact that the larger community within which it existed was housed by people who were looking for the spiritual environment of a Program Congregation.

With this awakening and a vision of deliberateness, the congregation began to design a plan for completing its transition so it could meet the needs of the populace that surrounded it and move past its years of languishing. Out of this deliberateness, a new atmosphere of welcome was generated for those who were exploring from the surrounding community.

Conclusion

A congregation, no matter how dynamic, will not attract those newcomers who feel no emotional connection to its spiritual environment. Like every other decision in life, if uncoerced, people will opt for their emotional preference.

There are different kinds of space within the spiritual environment of a congregation's life. If newcomers are to feel welcome then all of these kinds of space must be open at the same time.

18

Governing Principles

In conclusion, it might be worthwhile to review some of the principles that govern the life of voluntary religious institutions as a reminder that the characteristics of congregations of all attendance sizes are grounded in some common denominators that also determine success and failure.

Mission

Principle: **The ultimate social power of a congregation is commensurate with its measure of focus on its religious mission.**

This focus involves clarity of the mission, leadership investment in the mission, organizing around the mission, and devotion to the mission. Irrespective of the congregation's written documents, declared intentions, or public declarations, its true mission is revealed by the greatest focus of its energies. Thus, if a congregation wishes to know what mission it is really fulfilling this is where it must look.

Ministry is everything a congregation does to fulfill its mission. The greater the ownership of the laity of the congregation's mission the more profound their commitment to creating a powerful ministry.

The transforming power of a congregation is weakened by

every attempt it makes to substitute its religious mission with some symptomatic ideal. Liberals seem to be easy captives of the illusion that the symptom is synonymous with the cause. For example, community spirit, social action, and political correctness are natural results of religious mission fulfillment. They are symptoms of mythic transformation rather than causes of social transformation. That is, they will inevitably follow the mythic transformation induced by religious mission fulfillment. Thus, it is possible to foster institutional impotence in the attempt to give support to worthy symptomatic ideals when such ideals are substituted for the causal power of religious mission.

Community

Principle: **The most profound form of community is created by a common commitment to a noble and transcendent purpose.**

A subtle trap awaits those for whom community is the primary criteria for joining a religious institution. This trap is viewing community as an end to itself. It is natural, in a culture that is designed to alienate and create allegiance through false community, that the appeal of community would be so high and that the desire for community for its own sake should become a goal for so many people.

However, a community that exists for the sake of the experience of community leads a very precarious life. Since its members participate for the purpose of direct self-fulfillment it is consumer oriented and the strength of the community engendered is commensurate with the fragility of the egos involved and the group's capacity to minimize differences. It can only inspire a sacrifice that fulfills individual member goals. It is forever tied to the satisfaction of this conglomerate of self-centered needs for its success. Thus, it can never rise above this baseline of member needs. It remains a psychological whirlpool that sucks all expressed energies inward.

On the other hand, community that is bonded around an "outside our own skin" purpose that partakes of nobility creates the most profound form of human bonding. This form of community is a by-product rather than a goal. Its bonding is able to transcend ego fragility and lesser differences. It empowers the spirit of sacrifice with a concern for the needs of others because its primary makeup is by individuals with a group agenda whose fulfillment is outward. Thus, its energies can easily be invested in an outward focus whose investment, paradoxically, creates a new energizing of the community's life.

The essential difference in the bonding power of these two approaches to community can be likened, metaphorically, to the difference between the weakness of flour paste and the strength of crazy glue.

A peculiar characteristic of liberals is their deep desire for profound community while, at the same time, their will to succumb to a kind of individualism that tends to opt for community's weakest form, community for its own sake.

Growth

Principle: **If a congregation is fulfilling its mission it cannot stop growing.**

Congregational growth is not a goal, rather, it is a consequence. While there may be a deliberate game plan that entices growth, the greatest and most lasting growth always comes from a game plan that enlists its members in the cause of its mission. Usually, the major obstacle to such growth is a facility that cannot embrace numerical expansion. Thus, a mission-vital congregation is always concerned about how it can accommodate growth to its facilities, expand to new facilities, or begin new congregations.

Congregations concerned about how they can attract new members are not mission-vital. And congregations that seek to induce growth artificially through growth plans will only find temporary success through novelty.

The only factor that will obviate this institutional principle is some natural inhibiting circumstance of the physical, geographic, or social environment in which the congregation resides.

Institutional Power

Principle: **The greatest power to create social change derives from a common commitment to a common focus.**

The power to provoke dialogue through difference, to honor debate through challenged position, and to inspire creativity through openness is found in diversity. The power to provoke change through the power of gained attention, to highlight values through combined resources, and to appeal to social conscience through concerted behavior is found in unity. Diversity promotes tolerance and creativity. Unity promotes focus and awareness. While diversity may demand social appreciation for differences, it is only unity that demands social change through commonality.

There is nothing wrong when a congregation honors its diversity by celebrating its provocative dialogue, its embracing tolerance, and its unbounded creativity. These all speak to an inviting internal nature. However, if a congregation wishes to create social change then it must give stress to those commonalities that pay homage to its numbers, call attention to its values, and demand consideration of its voice. These all speak to a compelling external power.

Members may be made comfortable by a congregation's inviting nature of diversity but society is only changed by the challenge of a congregation's power of unity. The wise congregation does not permit itself to become enamored of one over the other. Rather it uses each to strengthen the other toward a wholeness that further enhances its capacity to create personal and social transformation. That is, it knows that neither is preferable to the other and that only both make for fulfillment of mission.

Still, it remains that the power to change society resides in the power of common commitment to common focus. For Unitarian Universalists, then, if the mission goal is social transformation then the phrase that best describes its social posture is diversity in unity.

Phenomenon Power

Principle: **Power shared is power multiplied.**

Power is a phenomenon that is both definable and elusive of definition. That is, it is something that humans can inevitably recognize, but they may or may not be able to identify its ingredients.

One way of defining power is as increments of attention. The more increments of attention an individual or an institution can garner to itself the more powerful it has become. Such power has to do with the capacity to expose individual and group values and messages to a larger group of listeners who might become their carriers. The greater the exposure the greater this possibility and, thus, the greater the potential power to influence social behavior and attitudes.

Another way of defining power is as life force. Life force is the spirit that emanates from each of our beings. Most of us have normal life force called personality, which we enhance through spoken words. Some people have such personality force that their presence is felt even without spoken words.

Yet another definition of power is the capacity to make certain decisions or behave in certain ways on behalf of other people that are granted by virtue of social position. Social, in this respect, refers to two or more people.

However we choose to define power, the notion that when we share it we multiply it still stands. Whether we give permission to others to receive the attention afforded us or to draw energy from our being or to perform position functions assigned us, we are sharing power. And whenever we share power another phenomenon occurs, namely, that our power, by virtue of its incarnation in another person, is multiplied. When power, whatever its nature, is transferred from one being to another it is infused with the power of the being with whom it is shared. Thus when the carriers of power are multiplied the power they carry is multiplied.

What this means is that power is not a commodity that we must hoard because it is limited in quantity. It is a multipliable phenomenon that can be increased by merging it with other existing power. And the reason it is unlimited is that the human well from which it derives, whatever its manner of expression, has the capacity to continuously generate what it is emitting.

Naming

Principle: **The power to name the solution is inherent in the power to name the problem.**

The universe's gift to humans is the ability to create meaning and, thus, to initiate the power to communicate. Inherent in this ability is the capacity to amass wisdom. A Chinese proverb recognizes this power by asserting that the beginning of wisdom is the ability to name. This power is metaphorically recognized in later western Hebrew scriptures when, in the book of Genesis, God grants Adam the power to give name to things.

The bottom line to the power is that, as meaning-makers, we humans can create both the problem and the solution. It makes no difference which comes first. Each is inherent in the other. Thus, when an institutional problem rises, the power to name a solution resides in the very power to name a problem. Equally, the power to name a problem lies in the very power to name a solution.

Again, humans remain capable of empowering themselves in every area of living related to social existence.

Anonymity

Principle: **The larger the attendance at the Sunday morning worship experience, the greater the potential anonymity of those attending and, thus, the greater the corresponding need for mission motivation.**

Anonymity is a place of hiding from the demands of institutional existence. It is an oasis where individuals become congregational ciphers. Anonymity also provides opportunity for people to do nothing but receive and such denies the grander blessing that comes from giving. This means it can be a place where the curse of self-centeredness finds easy expression.

Only a strong spirit of mission motivation is capable of empowering attendees to overcome the temptation of hiding in anonymity, to engage those gifting opportunities that redeem life from the estrangement of self-isolation, and to be a supportive part of the congregation's ministry.

In brief, the curse of anonymity prevails to the extent that mission motivation fails.

Value Survival

Principle: **The only values that survive the destructive forces of history are housed in institutional carriers.**

Institutions are society's value carriers. Their purpose is to protect, nurture, celebrate, and perpetuate a certain set of values. This set of values reflects a specific institutional mission. Examples are educational, financial, political, governmental, business, religious, etc. Values that are not housed in an institutional carrier do not survive the destructive force of social pressure and mythic conflict.

The principle of the survival of the fittest applies. The fittest is that which is able to adapt to the changing demands of its environment. Thus, it is only the fittest that has a continuing longevity. As an individual human, while I am alive, it is my physical being that copes with the demands of environmental change and serves as the carrier of my values. However, institutions, as groups of people, have a fittest capacity that far exceeds that of the single individual. The lesson is that if I, as an individual, wish the values I cherish to survive my body's demise, then I must invest my resources in an institution that, by virtue of its fittest capacities, can guarantee their continuing perpetuation.

Another lesson is that all of the resources I expend seeking to initiate and sustain social change will come to naught unless those resources are supportive of institutional carriers whose values are reflective of the change I seek. Further, any institution worthy of my resources will be committed to those wisdoms and dynamics that create the kind of power that impacts the social order. Such an institution is always a live, attention-getting drama.

Membership Meaning

Principle: **The greater the demands a congregation places on entry into membership, the deeper the level of commitment of those who join.**

This principle addresses the level of value the congregation places on its religious mission. In turn, those joining tend to equate their own level of valuation with the congregation's valuation. Aside from the internal value the individual brings to membership entry, there is no other valid criteria for gauging the degree of commitment the new member should bring to the act of joining other than those the congregation decrees.

The issue of valuation is normally approached in reverse by the liberal congregation, which makes minimal demands on membership because of its desire to be tolerant and welcoming and to affirm the worth of every seeker. That is, the liberal congregation tries to raise the level of valuation and commitment of its members after the act of joining rather than before. The consequence is usually a large peripheral membership of the minimally committed with a corresponding minimal motivation and support of the congregation's ministry. The question, which rises from this reversal and this consequence, is whether the spirit of welcome, tolerance, and worth affirmation are, themselves, minimized by membership demands of low-level valuation?

But, in whatever ways liberals may tend to ignore or reverse this principle, the history of voluntary institutions maintains its historical validation.

Vision

Principle: **The larger the body participating in the creation of a vision, the less the energy and time is necessitated for persuading a buy-in by the rest of the community.**

This principle is compounded as a congregation grows in attendance size. The opposite of this principle is equally true: the smaller the body participating in the creation of a vision, the more energy and time is necessitated for persuading a buy-in by the rest of the community.

This also underscores a parallel reality. One of the qualities of motivating leadership is the capacity to think independently. And people who think independently take more convincing when they are not a part of the originating creative process.

Communication

Principle: **The larger a congregation grows in membership the greater is its need for communications that are deliberately timely, focused, and pervasive.**

Smaller communities can rely on a chain of gossip and a spirit of family inclusiveness that keeps the communication active. This facilitates the spread of news in a fashion geared to necessity.

Larger communities quickly lose both this chain and this motivation except in smaller more intimate circles within its broader membership. With this loss comes an imperative of ministry success, namely, the deliberate creation of mechanisms of communication that reach every member in a timely, pervasive, and focused manner. Without this kind of communication, the congregation will lose the support of its members to those institutions that do have effective communication systems. An effective system:

- motivates commitment above competing claims for energy and time
- is timely in that it is an immediate reminder of opportunity for busy and burdened people
- is expressed in a form of quality that reminds of the seriousness of the congregation's mission

In a world where members are busy with multiple demands and whatever is immediately before them tends to become their priority, "out of sight, out of mind" is the order of the day. A congregation that hopes to compete with such demands and immediacy must rely on a system of communications that inserts itself into its members' weekly life as a prioritized priority. Otherwise, it will lose its voice to louder demands.

Space

Principle: **Available space will place a natural limit on a congregation's attendance growth.**

In this principle the key is attendance growth rather than membership. It is possible to have limited space and still grow in membership as long as those who are compelled to attend have room to attend. The requirement that sustains such growth under the constraints of space limitation is that membership either be revolving or disappears into a body of preexisting inertia or both. Thus, a congregation can have a continuing membership growth while its attendance remains static.

While a momentary spike in institutional excitement may temporarily obviate this principle, it will eventually prove true.

Attraction

Principle: **That which is most likely to attract new members is a sense of shared value and emotional commitment.**

This principle is honored in the adage "Birds of a feather flock together." A sense of group safety, security, and empowerment lies in such mutual attraction.

Behind this principle is the reason why most people join the ministry of a religious institution. They wish the safety, security, and empowerment that comes from joining with those who dominantly see reality as they see reality and whose emotional tone they find consonant with their own, irrespective of other differences.

When opposites attract it is usually for one of two basic reasons. One is because people are looking for the fulfillment of personal deficits and decide to acquire them externally. The other is the desire to deliberately relate to an opposite as a challenge to one's own growth.

Thus, while the attraction to opposites can be either a dependent or challenging experience, the attraction of commonality is the most likely reason why people join the religious institution. Therefore, it is not the size of the population in which a congregation exists that indicates its potential, rather, it is the size of that portion of this population that might hold common views and have an emotional identification with its expressed public ministry.

Ministry Appeal

Principle: **Congregations that grow in membership gear their ministry to the peculiarities that dominate the larger community in which they exist.**

The function of ministry is to couch the good news the congregation has to offer in the mode of the nuances of the culture it is seeking to serve.

That which appeals to people is an institutional ministry that reflects their own cultural makeup. If this community makeup is of a certain ethnicity or a certain social background then the successful congregation will be appealing to these eccentricities through its media image, its public worship experience, and its ongoing program. Kind appeals to kind. Nuance appeals to nuance. It is the same principle that governs the effective translation of one language into another.

Congregations that understand this principle will be able to apply their resources in fulfilling ways while avoiding the frustration that comes from being driven by the guilt of values that might be non-applicable such as ethnic diversity and political correctness. For example, it is a futile goal and an artificial vision to seek the achievement of an ethnically diverse membership if the community in which the congregation exists is not correspondingly diverse. On the other hand, this principle can be obviated by busing.

Quality

Principle: **Whether person, program, or product, people are most compelled by their attraction to quality.**

People are attracted to quality because it speaks to the best and people wish to invest their energy and resources in that which is superior. The best hints at that which transcends the norm and implies longevity. Thus, if a congregation is to attract the best possible members who will commit with the best that is within them, it must attain to the highest quality possible in fulfilling its mission through its ministry.

This notion of quality is counter to the typical approach made by Nominating Committees in their attempt to fill all the positions required to have an effective ministry. This can be called the warm body approach. Whoever is willing to fill the position, irrespective of their qualifications or lack thereof, is normally welcomed into leadership. Quality ministry calls for convincing those who are best qualified for any given position to assume its responsibility for the sake of a ministry that reflects itself. Warm bodies are insufficient to address the issue of quality. Only quality addresses quality. And only quality speaks to a high-level valuation of ministry.

Whatever values a congregation may espouse as focal to its existence, the quality of its ministry will speak a message about the quality of its commitment to these values. And such quality relates to everything that makes up the ministry package as a whole: programs, products, atmospheres, and buildings. People are normally not enamored of a disconnected message.

Spiritual Growth

Principle: **The larger the congregation the greater its reliance on faith development programming to maintain vitality and member commitment.**

Focal to faith development programming is the weekly worship and children and youth religious education event. It is this event that is the singular constant touchstone for the membership in the larger congregation's life. And it is the one event of contact for a significant percentage of this membership. Thus, this event must be highly provocative of religious growth and mission commitment.

Supporting this Sunday program must be a dynamic adult faith development program that offers depth of spiritual growth beyond the limitations of the weekly worship and education event. While the weekly service and education event provide the broad strokes that give outline and shape to spiritual life, the adult faith development program provides the short strokes that fill in this outline and shape with depth and color.

Larger congregations with powerful ministries always have a strong weekly and ongoing faith development program that fosters personal transformation, mutual support, and spiritual vision. This program is the heart of its spiritual ministry.

Social Transformation

Principle: **Social symptoms are only changed by changing the social heart that produces them.**

Vast amounts of time, energy, and resources are expended by Unitarian Universalists in what is called social action. Normally, the focus of this expenditure is to change social behavior. But while the goal and the efforts are noble the desired effect is usually negligible. The reason is that while it is important to respond to harmful social behavior such responses do not normally address the cause of this behavior.

Social behavior is a reflection of the social heart. The social heart is the distilled values of those beliefs held dear by the cultural mind. It is the heart that is the user. Therefore, if there is a wish to change social behavior and an expectation that the change be lasting, the social heart must first be changed by changing the beliefs that make up that heart.

Social action that responds to social behavior is important because it performs two vital services. It addresses an immediate need and it raises social awareness about the necessity of change. However, this is only a half step in the right direction. The completing half step is a message of transformation that offers itself as a replacement for those beliefs of the cultural mind that produced the harmful behavior. Such a replacement transaction alters the social heart and offers a corresponding alteration of those symptoms it reflects. The first half step without the second half step becomes an unending battle that can only consume resources without ever being won. The formula for social transformation involves equal commitment to both half steps. In brief, social action unaccompanied by a transforming theological message tends toward the ultimate ineffectiveness of the metaphorical finger in the dike.

Viscosity

Principle: **The larger the congregation the greater the necessity of small group and rapid-process decision making if effective ministry is to prevail.**

Viscosity refers to the thickness or thinness of a liquid that affects its capacity to flow. Metaphorically, the larger the congregation the thicker is its liquidity of decision-making processes. If the decision-making process in a smaller congregation is analogous to the viscosity of syrup the decision-making process in the larger congregation is analogous to the viscosity of molasses. Thus, with growth in attendance size comes the necessity of reducing the impediments which attendance size imposes on decision making and streamlining those processes that increase the speed and efficiency of decision making. This requires both reducing the size of decision-making bodies and increasing their capability of rapid response. That is, the natural thickness of the liquidity of decision making in the larger congregation must be deliberately thinned if ministry is to be effective.

Without such a shift in the means of decision making:

- The institution becomes captive of the process of micromanagement.
- Decision making becomes mired in this micromanaging style.
- Decision making necessitates maximum energy to produce minimum results.

A corollary principle is that the larger the congregation the greater the need for mutual trust in the decision-making process among both leaders and members. Such trust can only be instilled by mutual commitment to a common mission and by instituting policies that govern the behavior of the whole.

Cells

Principle: **Embracing members into vibrant internal cells of mutual interest is the only guarantee of a congregation's capacity to retain them within its drama of invested commitment.**

The larger the congregation the greater is its need for mutual interest cells that embrace members within its total body. The alternative is a fracturedness of investment and interest of its membership. Members who feel embraced in the congregation's community are much more likely to expand their commitment toward involvement in the nitty-gritty work that sustains the congregation's organizational life. The natural sequence is embrace first and involve second. The singular bonding agent that is capable of holding this multi-celled body together is a mutual commitment to a mission that transcends the interests of the individual embracing cells.

Again, the tendency of liberals is to reverse this principle by its approach of seeking involvement first and hoping that the involvement will somehow create an embracement. It is not a formula that touts large numbers of success stories.

Partnership

Principle: **Partnership is a way of relating rather than a way of organizing.**

While some ways of organizing may promote a sense of equality in partnership, its essence transcends such mechanisms. History exposes us to a critical truth about human community: the larger the group the greater the requirement of hierarchical levels of responsibility in order to achieve their purpose in a non-wasteful manner. The existence of such hierarchical structures neither denies nor affirms the spirit of partnership.

Partnership is an attitude that confirms mutual worth, the value of varied skills, the creativity of provocative conversation, and the power of common vision. Hierarchy of responsibility is only a way of processing partnership in an effective, focused, and energy-conserving manner, which designates multiple authorities for performing critical tasks. Partnership is a spirit rather than a function. Even though a task may be functionally organized as a partnership it is only a partnership if so informed by spirit. The manner of organization, then, is neither an arbitrator nor guarantor of partnership. Only the spirit of partnership guarantees and arbitrates partnership.

Abundance

Principle: **Those who see through the eyes of abundance contribute more because they see more to give.**

Nothing is more debilitating in human experience than a philosophy of scarcity because it reduces hope to impossibility and motivation to parsimony. Thus, it is the harbinger of failure.

Conversely, nothing is more invigorating in human experience than a philosophy of abundance because it enlarges hope to possibility and motivation to generosity. Thus, it is the harbinger of success.

The availability of resources has no bearing on the choice of giving level between these two philosophies. Those with equal resources will contribute at consequentially different levels if they see through the differing eyes of scarcity and abundance. The level of contribution will match the eyes that are seeing. It is the heart that is both the chooser and the user, and the heart is our values distilled into life focus. Therefore, a congregation that chooses to approach its resources in the spirit of abundance will always have as much as it needs to make progress in fulfilling its vision. This is the magic of abundance.

How does a congregation know when it has arrived at a philosophy of abundance? An abundant vision of possibility established as its goal in ministry reveals an underlying philosophy of abundance toward resources. Amply expressed attitudes of possibility and generosity of spirit are also attitudes reflective of a spirit of abundance. The bottom line is that a philosophy of abundance is not a phenomenon isolated to resource application, rather, it permeates the entire life of the institution and will find expression in its every sphere.

No congregation succeeds without achieving that shift in how it sees reality from scarcity to abundance.

Leadership

Principle: **Leadership makes everything happen that is going to happen.**

Whether it is one person or a thousand persons, if there is to be direction and movement toward happening, it will be modeled first by leadership. Inertia is the alternative, for which leadership is also responsible. Thus, whether it is action or stasis, leadership will cause it to happen.

Therefore, the issue is normally not a lack of leadership in institutional life, rather, a question of the type of leadership that either already exists or is needed.

Debt

Principle: **Where there is no institutional debt there is no institutional vision.**

Powerful growing congregations always have spiritual visions that outstrip their immediate levels of resource availability. Such institutions, because of their visionary character, refuse to allow resource limitations to dictate their ministry actions. Thus, these institutions will inevitably be in financial debt as a means of fulfilling their visions in a more complete fashion.

For such institutions there is neither a fear of being in debt or a pride of being in debt. Their attitude toward the acquisition of money is simply a natural stewardship response to vision motivation. Indebtedness, as a source of income to such congregations, is as legitimate a means for the fulfillment of mission as is a resort to pledge income or gifted resources.

Synergism

Principle: **You cannot do just one thing.**

This principle is endemic to the nature of the universe. It is inherent in the notion of an interdependent web of existence. It governs both the macrocosm and the microcosm.

Thus, what humans create can find no exception to this principle. Therefore, when one change is made in institutional life, all other elements of the institution will be affected, howsoever remotely. In this perception of effect there must also be a compensating one of adjustment toward synergism or the institution will suffer from internal dysfunction.

Since the universe just is, there is no value associated with either change or the effect within its being. Value is the product of human meaning making. So, whatever the value, negative or positive, that is given such change or effect, it will be determined by the view of reality of the human making the judgment.

Addendum I

The Corporate Congregation

The primary characteristic that separates the Corporate Congregation from the Program Congregation is its abundance of resources by which to engage its mission and ministry. This abundance allows for adequate professional staffing, grandly designed ministry programs, advanced equipment, and inviting space for processing these programs. Thus, an addendum to this characteristic is the capacity to be creative about the delivery of ministry.

Many church consultants are not comfortable with the designation of this category of attendance size as "corporate." However, the use of this label is intended to suggest that this particular kind of congregation has the available resources typical of corporations as distinguished from typical volunteer communities. No one has come up with an alternative designation that has stuck across the board. However, some church consultants are beginning to refer to this attendance size as a Resource Congregation. I will use that term in the following observations because it has a more accurate metaphorical ring than the word "corporate." Indeed, the term "corporate" is, in my judgment, a counterproductive designation since the values the religious institution seeks to live by are so different in both purpose and resulting relationships from secular corporations.

The other issue, aside from appropriate designation, is where the attendance mark is that delineates between the Program Congregation and the Resource Congregation. Some current thinking tends to focus on between 350 and 400 in combined attendance. However, other consultants believe that further research will show this figure to be much higher. One such consultant believes it may eventually approach the 1,000 mark. Some compromise for discussion purposes might be between 600 and 800. If we accept this range, then, those Unitarian Universalist Congregations qualifying for designation as a Resource Congregation, from the standpoint of attendance, can easily be identified.

However, there is another consideration. The very term "resource" places a lot of weight on the capacity to engage ministry with a high level of financial backing. The typical low sense of religious mission, the rather profound spirit of scarcity, and the aversion to obligated commitments on the part of liberals as a whole all tend to reduce congregational income to far less than what might be the case in a comparable attendance-size Protestant congregation. Thus, the amount of budgetary income must be a major factor in determining if a Unitarian Universalist congregation qualifies as a Resource Congregation. Indeed, it seems far more important than attendance as a barometer, given its resource character. I perceive that such income must be well over a million dollars in order to make possible the staff, worship, program, and services needed for an impactive Resource Congregation. Not many Unitarian Universalist congregations would qualify in this respect. This is why I have pushed the attendance size upward as a necessity in our religious movement for a congregation to achieve this resource stature. After all, that is the intended purpose of the designation.

A typical Unitarian Universalist congregation, if it is vital and spiritually healthy, might have a pledge unit average of around $1,200 to $1,400. Suppose the attendance is 800 on Sunday morning and this attendance is broken down between 250 children and youth and 550 adults (maybe a membership of 900). And suppose the total of the pledging units is 600. Multiplying 600 times $1,400 would add up to $840,000. This congregation would have to have a significant income from other sources beyond its pledge unit average in order to even begin qualifying as a Resource Congregation.

Consider some of the requirements for achieving this designation:

- An outstanding facility that can handle not only the attendance but the programmatic needs of such a dynamic institution.
- A considerable-sized paid staff of both ministers and other professionals.
- A powerhouse programming in every area of ministry.
- A "knock your socks off" Sunday service that partakes of significant music and media backing.
- A creative means of assimilating members in terms of both action and giving.
- A senior Parish Minister of somewhat mythic proportions who has beyond the ordinary preaching capacities and high-level skills in binding the entire staff together in a collaborative approach to ministry.
- A permeated sense of religious mission acknowledged by visible programmatic expressions that are able to address social transformation in a causal rather than symptomatic fashion.
- A deliberately created and engaged religious identity that causes the congregation to stand out in the public eye.

In brief, those who attend the Resource Congregation will find themselves immersed in a sense of participating in a drama that is larger than life. Only consequential resources and highly skilled ministers and staff can provide this kind of planning and energy generation. And only an adequate and versatile facility can house this possibility.

Essentially, this means that those Unitarian Universalist congregations that would aspire to this kind of powerful Resource Congregation ministry will first need to achieve a powerful Program Congregation ministry as the logical step toward arriving at the larger aspirational possibility.

If we were to push the Resource Congregation's dynamics through the six defining cultural characteristics, it would probably look something like the following for Unitarian Universalists:

(1) Size of Total Attendance

The dynamics are governed by an attendance of 700 and above.

(2) Manner of Member Relating

Since it resembles a "Super" Program Congregation it will have a complex multiple cell structure and a number of internal congregations. Its attendance size will elevate the anonymity factor and the general sense of relating will be vague but prideful except in those smaller cells that provide a closer experience of community. Metaphorically, it might be similar to relating to members of a small town. While one knows one is part of a distinctive institutional entity with definable boundaries, one does not know all the people that make up this entity. Yet, one will still feel a sense of peculiar relationship and institutional identity, even with the encountered stranger.

(3) Style of Basic Leadership

The primary spiritual leader will be a Senior Minister who probably possesses an aura of mythic dimension. In addition, there will be a large complex of ministerial and staff leadership. This leadership will all be woven into a collaborative team by the Senior Minister. Many lay leaders will exist who take their cue for ministry from the vision and training provided by this professional leadership complex.

(4) Nature of Manifested Community

The sense of community will be diffused and grounded in participating in a larger-than-life drama. It will be framed against noble ideals with a goal of personal and social transformation. It is this idealistic goal, as dramatized in the Sunday morning worship in the midst of a mass of people, that endows participation with its sense of being in a drama that is larger than life. It may feel like being part of a huge crusade. It will have a quality of grandness that will substitute for the actual closeness of more profound forms of community. The deeper experience of community will be reserved for those who venture into the smaller network of programmatic cells.

(5) Structure of Reflecting Organization

Normally the chief executive officer, which is the Senior Minister, will give guidance to and empower other ministers and staff to be creative about organizational structures that can be devised without official sanction and which will promote programming of an independent nature. Up front to this guidance and empowerment, the Senior Minister will have a very influential relationship with the governing body of the congregation in applying the principles of need and creativity to the larger organizational structure in which this smaller devising occurs. The envisioning of necessary organizational structures for efficiently fulfilling the congregation's mission will not be inhibited by traditional views and will be facilitated by the abundance of resources available for their implementation.

(6) Locus of Decision Making

Decision making will be pyramidal in authority from the top down. At the peak will be the Senior Minister. Even if there is a governing body that is given wide powers, the mythic persuasiveness of the Senior Minister will dominate its attitudes and actions. Authority for decision making will flow downward from this peak to and through other ministers and staff and lay leadership.

Addendum II

Creating an Evaluation

If a congregation wishes to know where it is in reference to the Pastoral to Program shift, its basic leadership may wish to expend some energy creating an evaluation form that could be filled in by its basic leadership and even the congregation in general.

This evaluation form could consist of questions and a rating system geared to the basic differences between these two types of congregations as illustrated in this book. Such a creation would lend itself to taking ownership of the perceptions inherent in the shift as well as providing an instrument for assessing both the progress that has been made and the issues that yet need to be addressed in completing the shift. The results could be used, in turn, to create a deliberate plan for action.

The value of local leadership creating this instrument is that they must come to some measure of mastery of the differences in the two cultures and find common ground in this mastery. This, within itself, would put a perceptual foundation under the possibilities of the shift.

On the other hand, there are evaluating resources already created by church consultants in some of the resource books mentioned in the reference section of this book. These are also available for use in congregational assessments.

Addendum III

The Maintenance Mode Tragedy

We appropriately assume that maintenance is fundamental to an institution's life, as in effectively taking care of both recurring and emergency needs as they arise. However, a primary shift occurs in congregational life when its vital sense of mission is lost. The shift is from a progressive movement toward mission fulfillment to a regressive passivity toward minimal maintenance. Given a few years of existence, this shift can constitute a change in institutional lifestyle. This lifestyle can justifiably be labeled as a Maintenance Mode.

This lifestyle is characterized by minimal vision, motivation, commitment, voluntarism, resources, and energy. The ultimate concern of the lifestyle is to instill just enough energy into the institution to keep it alive. Thus, the heartbeat of the lifestyle is normally just above the threshold of being comatose. In some sense, the persistence of this lifestyle announces that its purpose is to prepare the institution for death. If anything, the lifestyle is a flirting with this ultimacy.

What maintenance as a lifestyle promotes is a form of hibernation that ranges, depending on time in the mode, from a light slumber that might be aroused with a rough shaking to a deep sleep that will require the trumpet blast for awakening. The inability of a congregation that is in the grip of a maintenance mode to arouse itself rests in the confusion the mode creates between being in a state of peaceful community and being in a state of energy starvation. The essential symptom is the same, namely, the desire to remain inert. There is another symptom of maintenance hibernation that is even more debilitating. It is a period of time in which the sharp edge is taken off of institutional perceptiveness and dulled to a level of obtuseness.

There are very recognizable symptoms that announce that a congregation has succumbed to this institutional mode of existence. And the longer a congregation stays in a state of maintenance the greater the possibility that these symptoms will convert into serious penalties relative to its future. Following are a few of these symptoms.

Wisdom

The congregation in a maintenance mode is usually in minimal interaction with the world around it, despite the fact that it may be sustaining the illusion that it is through some form of marginal social action programming. The end result is that the congregation is not engaged in a posture that might provoke the growth of institutional wisdom. And as long as the maintenance mode persists historically, the longer the congregation persists in this non-interactive and non-growth posture relative to the world around it. If we look at our religious movement's history it becomes clear that some of our congregations have been in this posture for countless years.

The consequence is that when a congregation awakens from this mode it will do so to a measurable level of institutional ignorance about its own dynamics. What has been going on in the cultural school of learning will have simply passed it by. And the tendency will be for the congregation and its leadership to make decisions consistent with pre-slumber wisdom. That is, its tendency will be to make unwise decisions relative to its future because they will be based on passé insight.

Membership

While all manner of dramatic population growth may have been taking place in the environment around it, the congregation's membership will have remained fairly static. It may have fluctuated up and down but the congregation will usually have retained only those who were comfortable with its state of easy slumber, a state that members will sometimes refer to as community comfort. It may persist for years in this staticness as the population around it continues to burgeon.

Some members, feeling an unease in this slumber, might wonder why something significant isn't happening congregation-wise in the midst of this external growth. However, the tendency of the general membership will be to remain unperturbed by such questions or, if posed, to be clueless as to the answer.

Maintenance Saviors

The congregation is not committed toward investing in anything of consequence beyond business as usual. That which motivates commitment is absent because the sense of religious mission has been reduced to a pile of faint embers. These embers are only sufficient to keep the institution's heartbeat alive. Thus, there is little energy available for all the necessary tasks that need to be done. The congregation generally succumbs to the warm body approach in order to fill its vital role needs.

A solution usually arises to this lack of available volunteers that on the surface seems worthy but which, in actuality, can pose serious future problems. Inevitably, there are those who are willing to step into the breach to fill these vital roles and exert energy to fulfill the role's demands. These people are generally welcomed with appreciation. If these same people express willingness to continue in this commitment year after year they will generally be applauded as devoted leaders. The congregation, feeling relieved of the energy-demanding burden of these roles, may permit a wide latitude of freedom to these members and, by default, allow them to make policies, even when such might be in conflict with their role function. The upshot is that if these members remain in these roles long enough they will become institutionalized within them.

The consequences of this institutionalization will come alive when the congregation comes alive. When aroused out of its maintenance mode through a new mission awareness, the congregation may need to move into different organizational structures with new supporting policies for maximum ministry effectiveness. And one of the biggest obstacles to doing so can easily become these institutionalized "maintenance saviors."

Any attempt to make necessary changes that affect the role or policies these members have created can initiate maintenance savior sympathy, stir up vivid anger over perceived lack of appreciation for the maintenance savior's past contributions, engender the ire of the maintenance savior, and foster campaigns of conflict mounted by clueless members. Major crises can ensue that could not only result in membership loss but also drain away the energy needed to initiate new congregational direction.

The sadness of the foregoing possible scenario is that those members who have stepped into the breach during the maintenance period are, as a rule, truly committed to the congregation's ministry, which is why they initially volunteered. And this commitment may simply have grown stronger during their tenure in office.

The alternative scenario is that the maintenance savior will be part of that leadership that has awakened and sees the need for those changes, boundaries, and new structures that outline a new future for the congregation. If this is the case then the congregation has avoided this potential costly penalty.

However, the tendency will be for the person, the role they are playing, and the decisions and policies they have developed to become fused in their mind with resultant issues of self-worth becoming attached to all change. It is this fusing and attaching that signals institutionalization. It also signals serious future trouble.

Change

Once leaders have found a level of comfort in the maintenance mode, their tendency will be to resist change, irrespective of how compelling supportive reasons may be. And if the congregation ever awakens to its possibilities and begins to institute needed changes, a number of these leaders will become advocates of staying in the comfort zone. One reason for this advocacy is that these will have been the primary leaders during the maintenance hibernation and all calls for change could imply that they failed as leaders or there would be no need for current change. To support change, then, would be to pronounce a negative self-judgment on the validity of their own leadership.

Given this threat, some leaders will never be able to separate their self-worth from such negative implications of change. Sadly, they will remain enemies of the progress of aliveness. The irony is that the very reputation, about their past leadership, that they are trying to protect will be diminished by such attempts because the past positive nature of that leadership will be buried under the present weight of their negative resistance.

A critical question that accompanies the maintenance mode lifestyle is: "Who owns the congregation's ministry?" The answer to this question is simple: whoever is willing to take ownership. And this will usually turn out to be a very small percentage of the congregation's membership. Moreover, as already suggested, those who do take ownership are empowered to shape policy and determine destiny. The maintenance mode is, in reality, a scenario where the majority of members relinquish ownership to a minority of members.

Organization

Since the status quo is the preoccupation of a maintenance mode, the organizational structure of this congregation will be reflective. There will be little desire to improve or update the ministry's organizational delivery system because there will be minimal vision of any such need. It is likely that the congregation may have been still growing in membership as it began its descent into the maintenance mode. If so, it is also likely that the congregation may have grown into another attendance size without recognizing that this was the case. Congregations that fit this scenario, because they are organized to process a ministry that is no longer a part of their culture, may be organized for failure.

But whether this is the case or not, maintenance perceptions, given the passage of time, will inevitably reflect a blindness about organizational dynamics and need that only further deepens the slumber quality of the mode.

Secularization

Since the congregation's mission is the only legitimate gauge of its success, failure, and behavior, and this focus is essentially invisible, the ministry agents making up the congregation's life will seek substitutes. That substitute most likely to be adopted is the complex of readily available corporate mentalities in which the members spend the bulk of their living. Thus, the world outside the religious institution, which the religious institution is supposed to influence toward value transformation, actually captures the religious institution by capturing the gauging devotion of its ministry agents.

The irony of this capturing is that, irrespective of what the congregation calls itself, for all practical purposes, it becomes a secular institution even through it is espousing anti-secular values. Therefore, it loses its power to transform both itself and the world around it because its gauge of living is actually supportive of that which it is supposed to transform. However, this tends not to be a concern of religious institutions that have permitted their sense of religious mission to be lost to the status quo.

Space

Since the maintenance mode congregation will normally have a static membership it will see little need to invest in facilities expansion. However, if it ever rouses from hibernation and re-engages its religious mission it will begin growing. The most obvious issue it will face in this growth is lack of adequate space.

Along with all the other mounting resource needs that it will have, this one will become paramount. Indeed, it may become a major catch-22 for the congregation. The catch is that it may need to grow in order to increase its resources sufficiently to build more space but will not be able to do so because it doesn't have the space to make the growth happen. This can be one of the most apparent penalties of allowing the congregation to slip into a maintenance lifestyle.

Aliveness

In the midst of the placidity of the maintenance mode existence, members of the congregation may occasionally feel the need for some experiences that assure that they are alive. That is, they may need a metaphorical pinprick that produces a reaction indicative of aliveness.

There seem to be at least two primary ways that members in maintenance mode congregations fulfill this need.

One is for those members who have the greatest sense of this need to place themselves in positions and attend those meetings that permit the creation of some minimal conflictual environment that illusions aliveness. A way of producing this environment is to engage in debate over how best to micromanage the congregation's affairs.

Another is to permit some issue of minor importance to take on major significance so that the ensuing conflict makes members not only feel that they are alive but actually engaging an issue of importance. The value of this approach in creating a sensation of aliveness is that once the purpose has been served, members can restore relationships by mutual agreement that it was all nothing more than a misunderstanding. This also permits a resumption of slumber as if a newfound peace had been engaged. That this sets up a game play that is designed to engage trivia as if it were of consequence is of no concern. The purpose of the game is to produce a momentary assuaging sense, howsoever false it may be, of actually being vitally alive.

Money

One of the primal issues that will constantly plague the maintenance mode congregation is money. It will never have

sufficient funds to meet its needs and will often have periods of
financial crisis that will result in draining its financial reserves
and further reductions in its ministry programs. The typical
way of addressing this low state will be to create all manner of
projects that will enable it to raise extra dollars from both its
own members and the general public.

However, if its facilities are properly located, the major
means of addressing this stress will be to become a rental agency
for its own facility. That is, it will ask the secular community that
surrounds it to support its internal religious ministry by con-
tributing money via space usage. If it can swing renting to some
kind of school that invites it to feel that it is providing space for
a worthy educational endeavor, this will help divest the rental
scheme of guilt.

As the years pass the congregation's budget will gradually
become "rental dependent." The ultimate penalty for allowing
itself to be lured into this dependency will become apparent
if it ever rouses from this state of maintenance to pursue
its reason for being. This penalty can be one or both of two
problems. One is having built up such a heavy dependency on
rental income that it will require countless years to overcome
this burden. Thus, the monies needed to do adequate ministry
will be forfeited to overcoming this rental dependence deficit.
The other is that its space will have become the captive of its
renters and, thus, its own program will suffer in diminishment
from lack of space adequacy.

The mentality engendered by the maintenance mode is that
of a financial impoverishment similar to that created within the
minds of those who battled the 1930s Great Depression. The
difference is that today's sense of maintenance impoverishment
is usually an artificial construct within a state of abundance. It
is a compartmentalization of illusion and reality. For example,

members may spend more on daily coffee than they do on their pledge to the congregation. They may spend lavishly on entertainment and vacations while claiming financial destitution during canvass time.

The consequence of this mentality is that the congregation will normally approach all financial crises with nothing more than a momentary fix and the problems of ministry lack will mount exponentially along with the crises.

One other consequence is worthy of mention. Whatever the state of the congregation's grounds and facilities at the beginning of assuming a maintenance mode lifestyle, that state will usually reflect an attitude of impoverishment when the congregation finally awakens from its slumber. Band-Aid maintenance will normally have been the approach to facilities and grounds issues and, depending on how long it has been anesthetized, it is very likely that when the congregation awakens that its facilities will be in a shambles. That is, the message of its facilities will be that a destitute theology is driving the life of those who make up its membership.

Staff

Considering the almost total lack of vision characteristic of a maintenance mode and the profound spirit of scarcity that dominates attitudes toward money, it is hardly surprising that such a congregation's ministry will inevitably be characterized by a serious deficiency of staff leadership. This deficiency is maintained because there is not enough professional and trained leadership to cause things to happen beyond survival and, in turn, the fact that nothing is happening is used to justify maintaining staff deficiency. In brief, staff deficiency is a self-sustaining manner of being. And this sustained manner of being consequentially contributes to empowering the congregation's maintenance mentality as the standard for ministry performance.

Going *no where* sustains going *no where*. And history tends to confirm that the maintenance mode will persist without some form of leadership challenging its right to dominate the institution's existence. Yet, the staff of maintenance mode congregations can barely invent enough enthusiasm to keep their own spirits sustained, let alone produce enough to cause the congregation to wish to move into a new state of being. This is the maintenance mode congregation's biggest catch-22. And it traffics on the principle that leadership makes everything happen that's going to happen. Or, to say this conversely, leadership makes everything not happen that's not going to happen.

Normally, one of two things is required to break this mode open to the future. Either an outside consultant must come in with the capacity to inform, jar, and inspire. Or, a new kind of highly provocative leadership must be called by the congregation to sound the trumpet blast.

Aging

Consistent with its essential character, the excitement level of the maintenance mode is practically nonexistent. This lack impacts the kind of visitors who will return and possibly join. Kind attracts kind. And the kind of visitor attracted to the maintenance mode are those who are, themselves, invested in low-level involvement. This means that people who are younger in either age or spirit are not going to become enamored of membership in an institution that lacks energetic programming and vital mission orientation. Consequently, the tendency of the maintenance mode congregation is for its membership to gradually increase in age as younger people leave for more dynamic institutional relationships and older people take their place. Another characteristic of the maintenance mode congregation is a low level of institutional wisdom and, thus, the general membership will lament this aging process but will not have a clue as to why it is happening.

There is a corollary happening. If there are few alternatives as far as Unitarian Universalist congregations are concerned, committed people may still join. They will seek to instill enthusiasm and bring new ideas. But by and large they will only end up being sucked into the maintenance mode lifestyle. They will not like this but will remain faithful because their primary commitment is to the religious experience rather than to its specific congregational expression. Thus, the maintenance mode congregation's greatest negative contribution to the religious movement may be its draining of energy and vision from some of its most committed members who happen to have the misfortune of settling within the congregation's environ.

Jerry-rigging is an apt metaphor for the maintenance mode method of doing. To jerry-rig means to fix something as cheaply as possible. Jerry-rigging is a fix that disregards ultimate cost and ultimate consequence. And the ultimate cost is generally enormous and the ultimate consequence is generally disastrous. This applies to both the human and non-human components of the congregation's existence.

Beyond jerry-rigging, the maintenance mode is a style of deferring decisions that are critical to the institution's future. The bottom line, then, is that a congregation cannot stay in a maintenance lifestyle for very long without beginning to fall prey to its symptoms and potential penalties. And for Unitarian Universalists, this means becoming an inconsequential social club for pacified liberals.

Anyone who commits to awakening the maintenance mode

style congregation must be prepared with a spirit of patience and a sense of self-worth that cannot be challenged by misunderstanding, opposition, or lack of responsiveness. If jerry-rigging is an apt metaphor for the maintenance mode method of doing then Rip Van Winkle is an apt metaphor for the maintenance mode state of being. This congregation has drunk deeply of the blended elixir of benignity and comfort. History is passing it by. As previously suggested, if it has not been asleep very long, it can be awakened by a rough shake of the shoulder. But, if it has persisted for a time in this state then it will likely take an oft repeated trumpet blast to break through the thick haze of slumber that envelopes the congregation's whole existence.

The wise awakener will have a game plan that can be used to empower that edge of awareness that remains in those members who know something is wrong but cannot name it and who languish in a committed state of frustration. These are the people whose perceptive excitement must first be nurtured into becoming the lay vanguard of trumpeters. Even with this vanguard blowing with persistency, an awakening that happens within a year's period of time could be labeled as miraculous. However, the awakener should keep in mind that there is great spiritual reward for that leadership which is responsible for raising the near dead back to life.

What the foregoing does is place another shade of highlight across the notion that the entire destiny of the religious institution, irrespective of size, is bound up in its degree of commitment to its religious mission. Institutional dynamics do not permit exceptions to this insight. The maintenance mode is a basic institutional expression that operates with a decided lack of any influential sense of religious mission. Indeed, the conversion of its constituency into a horde of maintenance mode congregations may be the ultimate penalty a religious movement pays when it opts for a mission other than the one for which it was created.

Addendum IV

The Shift and Policy Governance

Over the past few years a new way for Unitarian Universalist boards to free themselves toward greater spiritual leadership in congregational life has been developing. It is a rapidly growing governance process in our religious movement.

Because it is based on a corporate model, its application to the volunteer religious community requires creativity. It is being used by both Pastoral Congregations and Program Congregations with genuine effectiveness. So it is not a model of governance that is exclusive to either attendance-size style. The reason it is applicable to both of these radically different ministry models is because it addresses a common need for the board to have more time to endow governance with the quality of visionary religious leadership and for the various agents of the congregation's ministry to experience a more creative empowerment for fulfilling their individual mandates.

A few observations about its governing characteristics are shared as an addendum to this book because of my own growing conviction that it models a form of congregational governance that is almost demanded for effective ministry to happen in the Program-size congregation. The ground of this conviction has to do with the complexity of organization, the multiplicity of decision-making foci, and the necessity of strong, committed lay spiritual leadership to keep the various seams that boundary aspects of the congregation's ministry bonded in spiritual unity and motivated toward mission fulfillment.

While the minister plays a large role in providing a single focus vision of leadership in the Pastoral Congregation, the grouping of lay-staff-ministerial leadership of the Program Congregation tends to fracture into multi-focused visions. Having a governing body that provides policy guidance based on the congregation's mission helps keep all components of ministry aligned.

What follows is not an attempt to delineate a full review of the policy governance model. It is only an attempt to outline some of its basic characteristics as a way of encouraging a more in-depth exploration. And while some essential elements of the policy governance model, as translated into our religious experience, are explained in the following, it is only one such way of outlining its basic directions.

Basic Characteristics

Authority

The board retains the ultimate authority it has been granted by the congregation to direct the congregation's ministry in the interim between congregational meetings. With this authority, the board removes itself from micromanaging congregational affairs in favor of governing through ends policies based on the institution's statement of Mission-Covenant. Thus, it becomes a policy governing body that ultimately establishes the boundaries of behavior for the total of the congregation's ministry. It is in the constant process of monitoring the various agents of this ministry as to effectiveness and need in light of these policies. While it is doing this it is provoking the congregation toward visions that will give direction to agent ministries and it is motivating toward the fulfillment of these visions.

Micromanagement

The board establishes an executive that meets as frequently as necessary to manage congregational affairs. In many congregations this executive is a team comprised of two to four members, inclusive of ministerial and lay leadership. In a four-member executive team a typical makeup would be two laypeople and two staff people (inclusive of the ministers) who would all have separate portfolios that cover the ministry life of the congregation. In large Program Congregations, the executive may be only one person. If this is the case it is usually the Parish Minister.

But, whatever the makeup of the executive, its capacity to meet when necessary and its small size makes it possible for it to both act with immediacy and deal with sensitive issues that a larger board might find difficult. The executive is governed by policies established by the board, reports to the board, and is subject to the board's leadership and visions.

Almost all administrative and programmatic agents of the congregation's ministry report to the executive, which is the conduit to the board for issues pertinent to policy governance or recommendations that relate to the authorities the board has retained outside those given to the executive.

Program

While the administration of the congregation is cared for by the executive, the program components of the congregation are normally cared for by councils composed of chief representatives of the programmatic ministry. Counsils give general direction to the program ministry of the congregation and address all related issues. Usually, a minister or staff person is assigned responsibility for helping such councils execute their responsibilities. The councils report directly to the executive.

Creativity

Organizational agents of the congregation's ministry are given a mandate but not a listing of how to perform this mandate. Rather, they operate by broad means policies that state the limitation of their authority. This opens these agents to the creation of lesser means policies that guide their own functions, and allows them to be as creative as they wish in fulfilling their part of the congregation's ministry.

Power

What the foregoing way of governance does is move power outward from both the board and the executive to the various agents of the congregation's ministry. This power relates to not only creativity, but also to decision making and self-guidance. The end result traffics on the principle that power shared is power multiplied.

It requires some immersion in the principles that govern policy governance to implement them into congregational life. And, normally, the board, already having the authority to determine how best to govern the congregation, does not go through a long tedious process of bringing the congregation around to voting on changing to this model. It is a waste of valuable time and resources for once the congregation experiences how the implemented model actually works and sees its profound values, it will applaud the board's wisdom.

This does not mean that a board converting to this model should not educate the congregation as to its structure and benefits. It should. But it should not permit itself to be seduced into allowing the process of conversion to be mired or stopped by the attempt of congregational members to do the very thing it is trying to extricate itself from, namely, micromanagement.

Any congregation that is making the shift from a Pastoral Congregation posture to a Program Congregation posture should also give serious consideration to making this conversion one of its primary goals.

One further consideration is important to note. For a board to claim to be functioning on this model is different from actually functioning on this model. It is easy for laypeople, whose living is spent in the corporate world, to process personal agenda and advance power claims in the name of this model without ever fully understanding either the model's function or intent. The purpose is not to further empower a board's micromanagement, rather, it is to remove itself from such management so it can lead through policy-based vision based on the religious mission of the congregation. A congregation genuinely interested in inaugurating this model must make sure that the board doing the transitioning is one invested in spiritual vision and mission fulfillment rather than the further promotion of private power agendas. It should also be certain that it has a clear and motivating mission statement upon which the board can base its policies, for this is the key to the entire manner of governance.

Caution: It would be easy for a board, converting its decision-making processes to this model, to do nothing more than intensify and broaden corporate mentalities that have already substituted themselves for religious perspectives. In brief, a board looking to explore policy governance should first look to whether or not the conversion will be based on a clearly stated sense of religious mission and relationship authorities grounded in religious values. To say this another way, the religious institution has a radically different bottom line and a radically different way of relating to both volunteer and hired and Called leadership than does the corporation. If the application of this model does not deliberately account for this difference it will do nothing more than continue the unfortunate reformation of our religious institutions into disguised mini-corporations with less and less spiritual power to help the world around it transform its values and relationships in some redemptive manner.

Addendum V

A Process for Developing a Mission-Covenant Statement

Introduction

Nothing has been more vexing in our religious movement over the past fifty years than the notion of mission. We seem to have been confused about its definition, wondered why it was important, replaced it with less controversial substitutes, or simply ignored it. Even when it has been given verbal weight, such seems not to have ignited our smoldering drama into flames. Yet, as other religious institutions in society will attest, it is the very heart of social success and the singular herald that determines destiny. That our religious movement seems to be on hold in reference to the constant increase in general population speaks to both a lack of measurable social success and a lackluster social destiny.

A Clue

Society creates institutions to fill its basic needs. That is, institutions are brought into being with specific missions in mind. Institutions that survive continue to fill those mission needs that are persistent in human experience. Aside from the family or community unit, the institution of religion was probably one of the first and has been one of the most enduring of social institutions. Obviously, its mission is central to the human story.

Back when humans sheltered themselves in caves, there was little to ponder except survival in a savage and terrifying environment. But then came art and language, and communities of meaning were born. Critical to making meaning were the compelling questions about the mystery of the existence of their environment. Yet, survival was a full-time commitment and little energy was left to pursue these questions. So there arose an institution in the midst of community, whose purpose was to enter this cosmic mystery and return with answers that gave meaning to human existence and direction to human community.

At first, this institution seems to have been a single person called by many names that eventually were recorded in various historical periods and cultures as witch doctor, shaman, priest, sage, imam, prophet, lama, rabbi, minister, teacher, etc. But, given the passage of time, this institution grew larger and more powerfully controlling and was given the name religion, which means to bind together, because that was precisely what its answers did for the community. So religion, and its answers to life's mysteries, became the holy enterprise, the sacred pursuit that infused community with its sense of meaning and purpose upon the earth.

However, as the human population grew and new communities were born and migrated and encountered other communities with different religious leaders and different answers to life's compelling questions of mystery, conflict arose over what was true and which community was its repository. Wars erupted over this contention because the answers to the questions of mystery remained as the soul of the human drama and people wished for both certainty and dominance in this quest for meaning.

Then, technology developed and made possible the spread of information. Ideological revolutions began to take place that threatened both the answers and the encompassing control of religions over the cultures in which they existed. As a result, an environment of living emerged that existed apart from the direct control of religion and its leaders. It began to be called the secular. Out of this came a new tension, the tension between the answers to the compelling questions of mystery given by religion and the answers to the compelling questions of mystery that emerged from the institutions of this secular environment.

As time passed and technological revolutions increased, so did the revolutions spurred by its information counterpart and so did the time available for individuals to pursue answers to life's compelling questions of mystery, which, within itself, was another revolution that spawned all manner of smaller revolutions. A significant part of the present world is the recipient of these revolutionary gifts of technology, information, and time. And, while institutionalized religion still plays a vital role in the human enterprise, its power has been ameliorated by all of these varied revolutions.

The reason religion remains vital is that the revolutions mentioned, rather than bringing final answers to life's compelling questions of mystery, have only increased both the profoundness of this mystery and the appetite for answers to the meaning of the human drama within it. And even when individuals feel successful in answering these questions for themselves, they also feel the need for the support of communities of affirmation and celebration. Moreover, the technological and information revolutions have yet to liberate a lot of the world's population and the religious institution remains a key factor for life instruction and direction in many of these areas.

The Questions

Out of this brief sketch rise several questions that serve as clues as to what might be the mission of the religious institution. One is: "What was the early primitive cave community seeking when it created religion?" To answer this question we must crawl back into this early environment and assume the cave community lifestyle. Another is: "What do all the world's great religions have in common that qualifies them to be called religious?" To answer this question one must strip away the actual answers that these religions give to life's compelling questions of mystery and look for common purpose. Within this stripping away also lies the answer to another critical question: "What is it that the world's great religions do not have in common that sets them apart from one another?"

Implicit in the answers to these questions is the mission of religion, however it may be articulated, whatever it may be labeled, or wherever it may find expression. In brief, every religion shares a common mission and that which distinguishes between them is quite apart from this mission.

Several other clues may help keep us from being sidetracked from the answer to these questions. One clue is that it seems obvious that the early community did not create religion in order to create community. Unlike people of today, who are vitally interested in an ideological community that is modeled on the extended family, the extended family life of our ancestors already existed and was given further bonding by desperate survival needs. That is, this tightly bonded community had a need beyond its own creation. It is this need beyond community that caused it to devise the religious institution. It is community that created and sustained the need for the religious institution and not vice-versa.

A second clue is that the community did not create the religious institution as a vehicle for social action. The only social action the creators of religion were interested in was survival in the midst of a bewildering and savage environment. It was something that made sense of the struggle humans were having within this environment. It was only when the human population grew and conflicts of meaning began to proliferate that the impetus for social action, as we know it in modern times, began to come into being. Thus, the direction that the early humans wanted for their community life was not how best to save the world around them; rather, it was how to save themselves within this world.

A third clue is that it seems obvious that political correctness was already inherent in the family structure of the clan community when religion was created. The clan could only have been looking for something far more significant than confirmation of such preexisting definitions when it decided to create religion. Moreover, it probably had insufficient social interaction with differing clans to make anything more than collaborating with them or winning conflicts over them as its concern in such relationships. Political correctness issues within and between clans awaited a later time and a more sophisticated form of social interaction to take on its cultural significance. It is possible that the insights the community was asking from religion were the predecessor of this kind of social sophistication. However, to suggest that the meaning of political correctness was the reason religion was developed is a conclusion that requires ignoring history, itself.

We do essential disservice to ourselves when asking the question of religious purpose outside of its originating context. But when we do ask it, to the best of our existing knowledge, within its original context, we will find an answer that has not lost any of its personal or social pertinence. And, if thusly sourced, it is very unlikely that any answer we come up with will traffic on religious mythic symptoms such as community, social action, or political correctness.

A Thumbnail Sketch

We have been so long without succinct mission direction in our religious movement that our congregational memberships have become housed by liberals who, oxymoronically, are heavily invested in the mission of their secular vocations but wonder why it is so important for their congregations. One of the reasons for this has to do with the infusion of this lack into the basic character of our congregations and the failure of leadership to grasp the seriousness of this oxymoron.

Following World War II, and on the heels of humanism becoming the dominant philosophy of our religious movement (1960s), we began to lose interest in religious mission. Endemic to this loss of interest was a growing desire to have no taint of Christian conservative fundamentalism rub off on our social image. To ward off such tainting, we began throwing away everything as worthless that hinted of this peculiar brand of religious fundamentalism. That is, we created our own brand of liberal fundamentalism, whose focus had to do with what was not true, as opposed to what was true. For example, whatever terms these conservative fundamentalists used, such as god, sin, salvation, grace, etc., we banned to a dirty word list.

And since "they" used the word church it was also consigned to this list, and we began to change our institutional designations to terms like society and fellowship. And some just referred to themselves as "congregations," rather than engage a fruitless debate over the use of any alternative designation.

Most consequentially, these fundamentalist groups kept referring to their religious mission. So, we began to deny that we were either religious or had a mission associated with religion. But this left us without apparent reason for being. So we began searching for justification of existence. Since there seemed to be a profound longing for community in our cultural environment, we became enamored of the notion that we existed to fulfill this longing. But being a community haven for frustrated liberals was not totally satisfying since we only seemed to appeal to a small segment of the population. Nor did community as purpose seem to touch on a depth of nobility. Thus, we cast about for some other reason for being worthy of institutional existence. And this led us to latch onto social action and political correctness as reasons for being that seemed untainted with fundamentalist religious perspectives.

However, having divested ourselves of religious mission, we faced a different problem. By what criteria could we judge our effectiveness as a "nonreligious group"? We were unwilling to make such a judgment based on how well we provided community or whether or not we generated sufficient social action or whether or not we fully engaged every social fad of political correctness. We needed a broader criteria that transcended the reasons we gave for our existence. And we found it in the corporate world. We imported the numbers game and efficiency criteria and used these as gauges. In brief, we plunged headlong into the task of secularizing our institutions, and this was encouraged by the corresponding secularization of our dominant theology, humanism.

But, all of this jerry-rigging of our institutions' reason for being left us hanging out with two primary issues. One was of a spiritual lack. This lack, in the vernacular of the time (1960s through early 1980s), was "inspiration." Everywhere this divestiture of religious mission occurred, our people were talking of the need for inspiration. But we had no idea what the source of this inspiration might be. We only knew that some basic motivational thrust was absent in our community experience. We only knew that despite our focus on community, somehow the actual experience of this community did not touch a sufficient depth as to satisfy our more profound longings. Moreover, this sense of community purpose seemed to have no central motivating nobility. And social action and political correctness were as impotent to fulfill these more profound longings as was our brand of frustration-based community.

The other issue was that of identity. Since we could not come down with certainty on any particular reason for our being other than that of providing a community haven for liberals who aspired to change social error, identity confusion reigned. By the turn of the nineteen-sixties into the nineteen-seventies, this issue had reached crisis proportion and our national headquarters in Boston set forth a contest with a cash award attached to its winning. The contest was a challenge for anyone to come up with an identity statement that would tell us who we were. It was a request for someone to answer one of life's most compelling questions, "Who am I?" from an institutional standpoint. Having lost our sense of religious mission we had also lost our social identity. Although someone won this contest and his statement was widely dispersed, it solved none of the issues that were pressing us about reason for being.

The Whole

In the 1980s, after a number of years of debate, we did manage to come up with a statement of principles and purposes that expressed some of the aspirations and postures of our larger association of congregations. These principles are a splendid and worthy statement of ministry. And there is a long list of sources of authority that cover every possible avenue so as to leave no potential Unitarian Universalist out. However, the actual statement of purpose at the end of these listings is a brief comment about the association's mission as a support agency for the congregations of which it is comprised. Despite the answer to the question of our association's purpose being relegated to this last paragraph, our congregations have latched on to the statement of principles that precede it as a kind of substitute for pursuing the issue of mission, assuming that such a statement of ministry facets and theological implications about authority are synonymous with a statement of mission.

While there has been progress made in understanding the need to define our religious mission, this progress seems minimal in terms of empowering our religious movement. We continue to wrestle with the issue of institutional identity and appear to have become satisfied with making this an issue for individual congregational concern rather than an issue that profoundly effects our entire movement, which is another negative symptom of its loss.

Confusions

This idea of the whole divesting itself of a problem critical to its well-being by investing its parts with the responsibility underscores another issue that plagues us. It has to do with the inordinate influence of individualism in our midst. The time-honored American notion of individualism seems to find perfect support in our views of free-belief and self-determinism. Here is the rationale that falls out of this influence: if this freedom of belief and self-determinism are to be honored, then each separate congregation will have to come up with its own sense of its mission. In brief, the philosophy about mission that appears to dominate our movement at this moment in history is that it is up for grabs by each individual congregation. From the standpoint of our whole movement, why society invented religion seems not to have any bearing on a definition of purpose for Unitarian Universalists. But such unconcern is a natural view of an institution that has separated itself as uniquely different from institutions that claim to be religious (another self-victimization of our radical individualism).

However, this divestiture raises other questions. Do we, in the present day, have the right to claim consistency of purpose with our heritage unless we, like our forbears, are driven by the same religious purpose that ruled their living? If we stand in a common stream of history, do we not also stand in a common stream of purpose? If they claimed to be a religious institution and we claim we are not, then when, why, and how was the basic alteration made to our social being? Moreover, what right do we have to use them as examples of religious commitment or as our roots in history? But even more important, if we do not share a common purpose with our ancestors, then what purpose do we share, and with whom do we share it? If we do share a common purpose with our religious ancestors, then we might find a clue to our present purpose by asking what was their purpose.

The bottom line is that we have, for many decades, given ourselves permission to allow our problem of identity differentiation from the Christian religious right to be confused with our reason for being as a social institution. And, in so doing, we have only succeeded in great self-delusion, the diminishment of our social power, and a slide toward cultural oblivion to overtake us.

The Ultimate Tragedy

Congregations that persist without an imperative sense of religious mission become victims of incestuous intrigue and iconoclastic illusions while their professional leaders become caretakers of impotent inertness and ingenious irrelevance.

A Critical Distinction

Even where there has been a rebirth of religious mission in congregational life, another typical confusion in the creation of our mission-covenant statements comes into play. It is the failure to distinguish between mission and ministry. Mission is simply a statement of reason for being. If succinct, it can be stated in a single pithy sentence. Ministry is everything that is done to fulfill this reason for being. Most so-called mission statements are, in actuality, long umbrella statements of various facets of ministry parading as mission or they are a diffused mission statement submerged within this sea of ministry alliterations. There is nothing wrong with a statement that says here is how we will fulfill our mission. What is wrong is confusing this listing with why the congregation exists. The difference is between "why?" and "how?"—between purpose and means.

The confusion between purpose and means not only dissipates the power of succinctness, it fosters another tenet of Unitarian Universalism that further diminishes the poetry of focus. We seem to subscribe to the notion that to be truly embracing of all, the concerns of all must be enumerated. Again, we allow the spirit of individualism to sabotage institutional power. Thus, the multiplicity of the facets of ministry normally listed in a typical mission statement is an attempt to be sure that no one's concern of ministry is omitted. In the end, such mission statements become less mission statements and more litanies of member concerns. They end up without the power of succinctness or the poetry of focus. They are uninspiring lists of diversity of concerns. Further, they simply perpetuate the illusion that means and purpose are synonymous.

It is not possible to create a meaningful statement of religious mission until the distinction between purpose and means becomes clear in not only our understandings but also our applications.

The Covenant and Change

Let us assume that a congregation understands the necessity of a mission-covenant statement to its existence and already has one. However, it was written ten years ago. This does not necessarily mean it needs to be rewritten, but the effect of cultural change should be weighed in reference to its sustained power to motivate the congregation.

Change in all areas of human existence remains unrelenting. The temperament of movements changes. Language and concepts alter meaning and become obsolete. New language and concepts come into being. In a liberal movement open to new perceptions of truth, theological perspectives evolve. All of this addresses the need for a mission-covenant statement to periodically become freshened to its current environment of living in order to sustain its power of motivation. What is up for grabs within the issue of change is not the congregation's religious mission but how this mission is articulated. This is where the creativity of linguistic power and poetry come into play.

Moreover, the people of a covenant may change as well as its environment of living. Group members come and go. As membership grows so does the number of members who were not part of the mission-covenant statement's original creation.

Assuming that all the criteria about linguistic and environmental change are in place, re-writing this statement will broaden its ownership and increase the membership's power of commitment to their reason for being. If nothing else, it will create a dialogue about reason for existence.

Values

A congregation without a clear and concise mission-covenant statement is like the proverbial ship without a rudder, its destiny will be chosen by the sea and wind of its environment. Conversely, a congregation with a clear and concise mission-covenant statement has that guiding rudder that empowers it to use the sea and wind of its environment to move toward a chosen destiny. It is the difference between being out of control or in control. This is a principle of institutional life that, like the law of gravity, cannot be defied without imperiling existence.

Church consultants translate this principle into a positive affirmation of the first three necessary ingredients of a powerful and growing religious institution:

+ a clear and inspiring statement of mission
+ a cadre of leadership devoted to this mission
+ an organizational structure designed to process this mission

In finality, a clear and concise mission-covenant statement empowers a congregation to:

+ understand its reason for being
+ know its identity
+ have a common focus
+ invest in nobility
+ experience one of life's most profound forms of community

+ keep its center stable during times of change, crises and transition
+ prohibit becoming the pawn of private agendas
+ give direction to its own destiny
+ attract members who share its sense of nobility
+ have a defining framework for the creation of visions
+ have a standard by which to gauge success and failure

Montaigne asserted that no wind blows in favor of a ship without a port of destination. And R. F. Mager suggests that if you don't know where you are going you are liable to end up someplace else.

A Model

Following is a model of a process that can enable a congregation to create a mission-covenant statement that invites all members to work on the same page. It minimizes private agenda, maximizes common focus, and avoids the confusion between mission and ministry. It is committed to the motivational power of succinctness and brevity.

Moreover, it is an attempt to ground the entire exercise in the firm conviction that religious mission is the heart of our reason for being and that this mission is not up for grabs. The only thing up for grabs is how this mission is articulated. In brief, this mission is not an answer to one of the questions about the mystery of human existence that calls for freedom of belief in its articulation. There is no mystery about why the human community created the religious institution. That "why" is easily discernable for those who wish to push history backward with the tools of information and logic. The only freedom is in how this "why" is expressed.

The Process Overview

A Process Committee is established to oversee and make happen every aspect of planning needed to carry through the process of creating a mission-covenant statement from beginning to end and to make recommendations to various responsible bodies relative to its education and sustenance.

The process begins with an educational phase that stresses the role of mission and covenant in the history of humans, the history of our religious movement, and the history of one's congregation. It is particularly important to underscore the role of covenant in a creedless religious institution as the grounding for identity and the role of mission as its statement of reason for being. This should included written material and editorials in the newsletter and a worship service devoted to this focus just prior to sign-ups for the kick-off workshop.

A congregational workshop is the next major event in the calendar and is the platform upon which the rest of the process is built. The reason it is vital is that it concludes with consensus statements of mission-covenant from the various table groups that comprise its organizational components. It is these consensus statements that will serve as the material basis for constructing the mission-covenant statement.

From the attendees of this workshop the Process Committee selects a Refining Team of five to seven people who represent the various perspectives and skills needed to create an inspiring statement. These perspectives and skills include a devotion to creating a mission-covenant statement, a lack of private agenda, the ability to articulate, and the capacity to be flexible and think conceptually.

The Refining Team, working with the workshop table consensus statements, creates a single statement. This statement is advertised by the Process Committee.

The next event is a series of cottage meetings (dessert parties), set up by the Process Committee and run jointly by itself and the Refining Team, where small groups of members (12–15) give feedback to this advertised statement to members of the Process Committee and Refining Team. It is imperative that at least one member from each of these committees be present at each of these meetings. The Process Committee member facilitates the feedback while the Refining Team member records the feedback.

On the basis of the feedback from these cottage meetings, the Refining Team revises its statement and the Process Committee advertises it again to the congregation. With sufficient time in between for the Refining Team to do its work, two additional all-congregational meetings (one and a half to two hours, generally on a Sunday) are held where this feedback and refining process continues. The final statement is then publicized by the Process Committee. On a certain designated date, at a called congregational meeting, this final statement is recommended for vote (up or down) and adopted. The up or down vote assumes that there has been ample time for dialogue and that the last thing the congregation, as a whole, either wants or needs to do is become involved in further wordsmithing of the statement.

This process, from kickoff Sunday to adoption (not inclusive of the educational period), normally takes about five or seven months.

Sample Timeline

Educational phase	Spring, summer, September
Kick-off Sunday service	Late September
Congregational workshop	Early October
Congregational cottage meetings	Two middle weeks of November
Congregational feedback meetings	January and February
Congregational adoption meeting	March or April

The Workshop

The workshop normally lasts around seven-plus hours, inclusive of continental breakfast, lunch, and appropriate breaks. Assume table groups of no more than six people (preferably five) with a facilitator who knows clearly her/his function and participates while facilitating.

Also, assume that all consensus exercises in the workshop, as processed through table groups, begin with silent time for the individual to ponder and write the assignment, move to round robin sharing of these individual statements (with a focus on listening for commonalities…no dialogue except for the sake of clarity) and proceed to the group seeking a consensus statement. These consensus statements are transferred to a single newsprint sheet and, in turn, presented to the entire workshop group and posted for all to see. Commonalities are then collated.

Following is a basic outline of the workshop components that experience designates as essential:

+ Review of the entire mission-covenant creation and adoption process.
+ Review of the history of mission issues in our religious movement.
+ Review of the values of a mission-covenant statement
+ Review of consensus-seeking guidelines
+ Achievement of table group consensus: "What was the original purpose for the creation of the religious institution?" or "What qualifies an institution to be called religious as opposed to educational, political, governmental, etc.?" Conclusions of the various groups are shared and discussed.
+ Review of Mission-Covenant Statement Guidelines
+ Various mission-covenant statements are pushed through the guidelines, both religious and secular (example: Preamble to the Constitution of the United States of America, the UUA Statement of Principles and Purpose, the congregation's last mission-covenant statement, statements from other UU congregations, etc.).
+ Table groups develop a mission-covenant statement through the suggested consensus process as guided by the mission-covenant statement guidelines.
+ Table group consensus statements are shared.
+ Participants indicate the commonalities that exist between the various table group statements.
+ Table group consensus statements are gathered for use by the Refining Committee.
+ Table group facilitators make private recommendations to the chair of the Process Committee as to whom at

her/his table might be qualified to be on the Refining Committee (this is done without consulting with those being recommended).

Mission-Covenant Statement Refining Team

The quality of membership of this team is critical to the success of the entire process of developing the statement. Its members must

- have stature in the life of the congregation; otherwise, they will not be accorded a seriousness commensurate to the statement they will be producing
- be flexible in attitude and conceptual in approach in the use of language; otherwise, they will take ownership of the statement in a manner that precludes responding effectively to congregational feedback
- represent both head and heart in wordsmithing capacity; otherwise, they will not articulate the congregation's need for the statement to be both succinct and inspiring
- not be threatened by negative response or susceptible to appeals for inclusion; otherwise, they will lose sight of the goal and create a meaningless monstrosity designed to satisfy all private whim
- be committed to following the same creation and limitation guidelines that the congregational members followed in creating the table group consensus statements

The Refining Team begins a series of meetings to create a single mission-covenant statement from the multiple statements that emerged from the workshop. It uses the same guidelines relative to the creation of this statement and the consensus-seeking process as used in the workshop. Its work is governed by the adoption timeline established at the very beginning of the entire process.

Sample Cottage Meeting Process
(Articulated by the Congregation of Princeton, New Jersey)

Cottage meetings are set up in specific geographic areas to make attendance convenient. The host/hostess have only the single responsibility of providing adequate and comfortable space, coffee or tea, and a nice dessert, all served in a manner that speaks to the importance of the event.

At least one member each of the Process Committee and Refining Team should attend each cottage meeting, one to facilitate and one to take notes.

Following are six suggestions for making the meeting as smooth and productive as possible with minimal conflict:

1. Review the purpose of the meeting (why we are doing this).

2. Review the calendar of the entire Mission-Covenant process (have copies available).

3. Review the process of the cottage meeting (what will happen during this time frame).

4. Distinguish between a Mission-Covenant statement and a listing of those facets of ministry that seek its fulfillment.

5. Review the Mission-Covenant statement Guidelines.

6. Address the facilitation guidelines for the ensuing discussion:

   ✦ Distinguish between content and wordsmithing.
   ✦ Think conceptually.
   ✦ Share without disputation; ask questions for clarification only.
   ✦ Let the sharing of others spark your own imagination.
   ✦ Disconnect your self-worth from your ideas and suggestions.

When deemed necessary, remind participants that the purpose of a mission-covenant statement is not to incorporate everyone's ideas; rather, it is to focus on the religious mission of the congregation as briefly and succinctly as possible and to state the membership's dedication toward its fulfillment.

You may wish to have 4x6 cards available for specific feedback from individuals so that the note taker is not totally inundated and so the meeting process is not slowed down. You will also wish to have all the materials used during the workshop available for people who did not attend the workshop.

And last, please take time at the conclusion of the meeting to thank the host/hostess and the participants for their commitment and input.

Mission-Covenant Statement Guidelines

Everyone at the workshop, at the cottage meetings, and all other refining meetings are introduced to and use the same set of guidelines for the creation of the mission-covenant statement.

A mission-covenant statement is boundaried by two related perimeters. It should contain:

1. As much information as necessary to make clear its intentions.

2. No more information than is necessary to make clear its intentions.

A powerful statement that actually motivates members is short enough to be memorized and inspiring enough to be advertised in a wide variety of ways as a reminder of why the congregation exists. Such a statement will rarely exceed seventy-five to eighty words.

Using this formula, following are suggested guidelines, which embody the essential components of such a statement.

Identity of People

The opening phrase of the statement should identify the people who are forming the covenant.

Question: "Who are the people of the covenant?"

Reference: What label distinguishes this people from all other groups?

Focus of Mission

Following the opening identity phrase, the statement should indicate the mission of the covenanting group.

Question: "For what purpose are the people gathered in covenant?"

Reference: Why does any religious institution exist?

Source of Authority

Where is the locus of authority for creating the covenant and pursuing the mission?

Question: "What governs and validates the group's existence?"

Reference: How does the group know what it knows?

Posture Toward Truth

In what manner do the people of the covenant relate to reality? Is their body of truth living or dogmatized?

Question: "What is the style of the covenanting group?"

Reference: Is the style open or closed to further truth?

Means of Fulfillment

The closing sentence of the statement should indicate how the covenant is going to be transformed into reality. This involves both an indication of the intentions of the covenanting group and the resource means by which this intention will be fulfilled.

Question: "What is the pledge of the group toward making its mission real in the world?"

Reference: What form and level of commitment binds the group to their common mission?

The mechanism of these five elements was developed by studying both past Unitarian Universalist statements and secular statements, such as the Constitution of the United States. It was first introduced at a district-wide training event in the late nineteen-eighties in the west. Since then it has been used by many congregations. Some of the reasons for its success are:

- ✦ It minimizes the insertion of private agenda into the process.
- ✦ It places everyone on the same page in respect to the elements of inclusion.

- It denies the confusion of making the statement a listing of facets of ministry.
- It creates a statement of social identity.

It is this last reason that is vital to the non-creedal religious community. Since our congregations have no defining dogma, the two elements about the source of authority and posture toward truth answer the most often asked questions about the nature of our religious experience. These two statements are bounded by the name of the congregation, the statement of mission, and in conclusion, the covenant about fulfillment of mission. Together, these five elements constitute a statement of social identity and become the congregation's primary means of publicizing its reason for being in the larger community.

The actual mission statement could be made in one brief pithy sentence, as it should be. But standing alone this state-ment has neither the authority source and truth posture con-nections nor the power of covenant commitment that the other elements provide which makes it a potential tool of institutional and social identity. Reading this statement, inclusive of these elements, will make clear the distinction between this religious group and all others in the cultural environment. This is of special importance since most western religious groups define themselves by theological statement.

Consensus-Seeking Guidelines

Characteristics

Consensus seeking is a higher form of community decision making than democracy because its attempt is resolution through concurrence rather than concession by vote. And it is made possible by a concentration on commonalities rather than differences, general concepts rather than specific definitions, and possibilities rather than limitations.

Thus, consensus seeking attempts to umbrella the community by being inclusive rather than exclusive and by being expansive rather than contractive. Further, it stresses agreement while avoiding argument and focuses on community building rather than community control.

While the goal is community agreement, it especially honors the individual through its attempt to hear every person's voice. Thus, it empowers both the individual and the community by virtue of common commitment.

Requirements

To whatever extent consensus seeking is achieved, it will become so because those involved pay heed to the following requirements:

- actively participating in the dialogue
- listening to the perceptions of others
- thinking in terms of flexible concepts
- seeking concurrence rather than dominance
- using imagination.
- separating individual worth from individual belief
- keeping the goal of mutual empowerment in mind
- remembering that consensus is not a vote

Frustration

Except in the smallest of groups, it is rare for a consensus process to end up with everyone feeling totally satisfied. And the sharper the statement requirement the less the likelihood that total satisfaction will occur. It is important not to allow frustration issues about inclusion or exclusion to divert the community from the goal that prompted the use of the consensus process. Following are a few observations that may help the community from falling into the trap of viewing the process as the goal.

- In the consensus process, which is selective by nature, it is individual decision that determines inclusion or exclusion.

- The decision of the individual to say no in the consensus process is not a negative reflection on the community's mission, integrity, or caring spirit. It is simply the individual exercising the prerogative of free choice. Individuals are best honored by respecting their no as well as their yes.

- Neither the worth of the community or the worth of the individual is affected by the outcome of the procedures of either consensus seeking or democracy. Worth relates to beliefs about the nature of humanness rather than the end result of dialogue processes.

- Neither the consensus process nor the democratic process is the goal of community. Process is a means rather than an end. It is the fulfillment of the religious mission of the community that is the goal. And it is the effect on this mission that serves as the criteria for determining when consensus seeking ceases to be a constructive use of community energy.

- The community must learn to live with the right of the individual to opt for exclusion just as the individual must learn to live with the right of the community to protect its reason for being by determining the limits of the consensus-seeking process.

- To jeopardize the institution's mission for the sake of a false inclusion is to deny both the consensus process and the democratic process in favor of minority control and

such obviates the very purpose of both of these decision-making processes. Further, it is to disempower the
community as the agent of the individual's redemption.

The key to addressing frustration in the consensus-seeking
process, to whatever extent such is possible, is to raise the level
of satisfaction of the participants as opposed to lowering the
level of dissatisfaction. It is the difference between focusing on
the potential and focusing on the problem.

Approach

The attitude by which participants approach the consensus-
seeking process consequentially impacts the outcome. A "hard
posture" approach will contribute negatively to the outcome. A
hard posture approach is characterized by a "this is where I stand"
attitude that creates a defensive response from those holding differing views and tends to preclude mutual agreement and view
expansion. The hard approach sees only pros and no cons.

On the other hand, a "soft posture" approach will contribute
positively to the outcome. A soft approach is characterized by
an "I am open to considering other ways of saying this" attitude
that encourages exploration and creativity. The soft approach
sees both pros and cons.

Moreover, the tendency of the hard approach is to inject the
dialogue with false notions about participant worth, while the
soft approach tends to dismiss such notions.

Resort

When it becomes obvious that the consensus-seeking
process has arrived at a stalemate, the community may wish to
resort to the democratic process as a way of bringing closure
to the dialogue. When a democratic vote is entered from the

foundation of consensus seeking, the end result will inevitably be a higher level of majority opinion. To resort to democratic vote does not imply failure; rather, it announces the limit of the consensus-seeking process and calls for a final accounting of the group's opinion.

Samples

United States Mission-Covenant Statement

We the people of the United States *(identity of the people)*, in order to form a more perfect union, establish justice, insure domestic tranquility, provide for the common defense, promote the general welfare, and secure the blessings of liberty to ourselves and our posterity *(focus of mission)*, do ordain and establish this constitution for the United States of America *(covenant—what follows is generally a statement as to how this mission will be fulfilled)*.

Mission Statement of the Unitarian Universalist Association

We, the member congregations of the Unitarian Universalist Association *(identity of the people)*, covenant to affirm and promote:

+ The inherent worth and dignity of every person
+ Justice, equality, and compassion in human relations
+ Acceptance of one another and encouragement to spiritual growth in our congregations
+ A free and responsible search for truth and meaning
+ The right of conscience and the use of the democratic process within our congregations and in society at large
+ The goal of world community with peace, liberty, and justice for all
+ Respect for the interdependent web of all existence of which we are a part *(values that inform ministry)*.

The living tradition we share draws from many sources:

+ Direct experience of that transcending mystery and wonder, affirmed in all cultures, which moves us to renewal of the spirit and an openness to the forces which create and uphold life.

+ Words and deeds of prophetic women and men, which challenge us to confront powers and structures of evil with justice, compassion, and the transforming power of love.

+ Wisdom from the world's religions, which inspires us in our ethical and spiritual life.

+ Jewish and Christian teachings, which call us to respond to God's love by loving our neighbors as ourselves.

+ Humanist teachings, which counsel us to heed the guidance of reason and the results of science and warn us against idolatries of the mind and spirit.

+ Spiritual teachings of earth-centered traditions, which celebrate the sacred circle of life and instruct us to live in harmony with the rhythms of nature *(source of authority and implied posture toward truth of a radical openness).*

Grateful for the religious pluralism which enriches and ennobles our faith, we are inspired to deepen our understanding and expand our vision. As free congregations, we enter into this covenant, promising to one another our mutual trust and support *(means of fulfillment).*

The Unitarian Universalist Association shall devote its resources to and exercise its corporate powers for religious educational and humanitarian purposes. The primary purpose of the Association is to serve the needs of its member organizations, organize new congregations, extend and strengthen

Unitarian Universalist institutions, and implement its principles *(statement of mission)*.

The Jefferson Unitarian Church, Golden, Colorado (1990)

We, the members of Jefferson Unitarian Church *(identity of people)*, are engaged in a free and open search for truth *(posture toward truth)*.

We seek enlightenment from human heritage and life experience and find inspiration in uniquely personal ways *(source of authority)*.

We covenant to live those transforming truths, which bring spiritual wholeness and harmony to personal, global and universal relationships and thereby inspire hope for the future *(focus of mission)*.

To this end we commit our combined actions and personal resources *(means of fulfillment)*.

Mission-Covenant Statement of the Unitarian Universalist Congregation of Princeton, New Jersey *(identity of people)*

We come together in a free and open search for meaning within the mysteries of life *(focus of mission)*.

We draw inspiration from the wisdom of the ages *(posture toward truth)*, guided by reason, intuition, and experience *(source of authority)*.

Transformed through our shared explorations, we are compelled to build a better world in harmony with all existence *(focus of mission)*.

We commit to love, respect, and nurture each other in our lifelong spiritual journeys.

We pledge our hearts and hands our minds and means to this sacred bond *(means of fulfillment)*.

The Mission-Covenant Statement and the Shift

Wherever a congregation is in reference to the shift from Pastoral Congregation to Program Congregation will be reflected in its mission-covenant statement. If it is just beginning the shift and a mission-covenant statement is created by the congregation, this statement will probably reflect the membership's unwillingness to let loose of the notion of community as its reason for being. If it has been beyond the pastoral mode of thinking and behaving for a lengthy period of time, this statement will reflect a different reason for being, depending on the most dominant influence of its recent years. For example, if the dominant influence has been social action and political correctness, this will find a consequential reflection in the statement. This, of course, is consonant with the prevailing notion in Unitarian Universalism that religious mission is up for grabs by each individual congregation and has nothing to do with either the history of our movement or the historic reason for being of religion, itself.

The problem is that such disregard of why our religious movement exists will continue to influence our institutional life until professional leadership decides that reason for being of an historical nature actually has something to do with the existence of current Unitarian Universalism.

The loss of religious mission in our movement is not inconsequential to the notion that Unitarian Universalists, in relation to population growth, continue to decline numerically. This seems to parallel the notion that this decline can find some of its roots back in the 1960s and 1970s when we resorted to secularizing our existence in order to create a social identity that was the opposite of everything that the religious right seemed to represent (religious mission, religious language, state of the art methodology, financial devotion, gripping vision, etc.). That the average age of the membership of so many of our congregations continues to rise speaks to this foundation. So, indeed, where there is no sense of religious mission, the purpose of our congregations is up for grabs, depending on majority whim.

Thus, in developing a mission-covenant statement, any congregation wishing to do more than simply reflect the idiosyncrasy of its membership's current majority perspective will, of necessity, be required to grapple with why society originally created the religious institution.

The Committee On Ministry (an Original and Workable Model)

Introduction

The Committee On Ministry is a concept that has been shaped in a multiplicity of forms. Sometimes the resulting form has worked and sometimes it has not. Thus, while the concept remains valid some of the forms it has taken have not lived up to the concept's potential.

The model that is presented in the following remarks is that of the originally envisioned Committee On Ministry. It worked for many years in a very effective fashion for the congregation where it was first inaugurated. While there are no perfect models, this one has been subjected to the fires of experience and proven itself worthy.

The Concept

The concept of the COM began emerging in the late 1970s. It was originally grounded in two concerns. Congregations normally evaluated the effectiveness of the professional minister but not of themselves. The implication was that it was the professional minister who was responsible for the success or failure of the congregation's ministry, rather than the congregation. This also implied that the minister, rather than the congregation, owned this ministry.

The existence of a Ministerial Relations Committee amplified the foregoing issues. Why should the professional minister have a relations team and not the congregation? Why would the professional minister need an advisory team and not the congregation? Why would the professional minister have an agent of accountability and not the congregation? Where, except in religion, is it perceived that the basic leader of an institution needs a relational advocate?

Moreover, the Ministerial Relations Committee tended to become politicized over issues and it, more often than not, became the professional minister's advocate. This diminished its influence when congregants began expecting it to take the minister's side, and consequently, its voice was accordingly discounted. Indeed, this committee often further polarized issues of relationship rather than aiding in their resolution.

This view also sees the issue of what the professional minister needs from a different angle. The minister does not need a lay support group within the congregation. Professional support should come from colleagues who understand the peculiar issues of professional ministry, can receive information in a confidential manner, and bring true empathy to the relationship.

What the minister does need in the congregation being served is a group of caring and open laypeople who will give honest and pertinent feedback and advice relative to the effectiveness of the ministry of the minister within the context of the congregation's total ministry. And, in turn, what these laypeople need is a minister whose ego is of sufficient strength as to be unthreatened by this advice. This is the purpose of the

COM's role in respect to the professional minister's part of the congregation's total ministry.

Predicates

Out of the previously stated sense of discrepancy of accountability and skewed relationship advocacy between the congregation and the professional minister came the following predicates:

- ✦ The mission of the congregation is under the congregation's own exclusive ownership.
- ✦ Ministry is everything the congregation does to fulfill its mission.
- ✦ The congregation is ultimately both responsible and accountable for the success or failure of its ministry.
- ✦ What is best for the whole of the congregation's ministry is what is best for those parts of the ministry that make up the whole.
- ✦ While the professional ministers and staff play vital roles of leadership within the congregation's ministry, they are servants of the congregation's ministry and are not its owners.
- ✦ There should be an agent in congregational life that represents the total of its ministry, that is responsible for monitoring, evaluating, protecting, educating, and advising in respect to its effectiveness and which is inclusive of both professional and lay leadership functions.

Such an approach to ownership places the responsibility for success or failure squarely on the shoulders of the congregation without diminishing the value or leadership of the professional ministry. Indeed, it enhances the capacity of the professional minister to fulfill her or his role by focusing on leadership qualities rather than the creation of symptoms of success.

Standard

The standard by which all facets of ministry are evaluated is grounded in the congregation's statement of mission-covenant. All statements of mission held by various agents of this ministry are secondary to this statement. If this statement is clear and powerful, so is the ground of evaluation. The reverse is equally true. And, since ministry is everything a congregation does to fulfill its mission, a mission statement that is basically a listing of various facets of ministry is not a mission statement and is useless as an instrument for evaluating ministry. Using a mission-covenant statement that is only a listing of facets of ministry to evaluate ministry is akin to using a symptom to evaluate a symptom.

Further, a mission statement that does not involve a covenant of commitment toward its fulfillment leaves little room for commitment expectation. Thus, while the effectiveness of ministry can be gauged against the fulfillment of mission, the accountability for this fulfillment lacks a basis for gauging. Accountability requires that the mission statement end with a covenant of commitment by the congregation's members. This is why the preferable language is mission-covenant statement.

Agent

The COM becomes the primary agent upon which the congregation relies to attain the highest possible fulfillment of its mission through ministry. This reliance involves a number of critical functions:

Assessment

The COM is responsible for working out a plan to assess the effectiveness of every facet of the congregation's ministry. Using a plan that annually alternates assessing the total congregation's ministry and the professional minister's ministry conserves energy. Moreover, survey tools and methods that vary from year to year, have brevity and specific focus that encourage response, and represent ways of assessment that encourage creativity, elevate both interest and response.

Whatever the rhythm, tool, or method used, a pertinent report should be made to the board of trustees and the result should be converted into specific recommendations made to specific agents of the congregation's ministry. Otherwise, such a report remains an inert entity unless, of course, everything is going so well that recommendations are not necessary. If so, this should be the report.

Although the COM may choose to make a periodic concerted evaluation of the congregation's ministry, it should be understood that assessing is a year-around activity rather than an occasional event.

Education

Since its assessments and recommendations are geared to the congregation's mission-covenant, it seeks every opportunity to promote awareness and engender higher levels of commitment to this purpose. This includes brochures, orientations, newsletter editorials, worship services, and reports to the board of trustees and congregation at its annual meetings.

Consultation

It is in constant consultation with the professional ministers as regards effective leadership and relationships. It encourages the ministers to establish annual goals that can be visibly measured. It makes recommendations to the ministers in respect to enhancing the quality of their leadership as well as recommending their Compensation Packages to the appropriate bodies.

It is equally in consultation with all the other agents of the congregation's ministry at those times which it deems appropriate and meaningful. Its sense of contact with the congregation's total ministry, aside from the professional ministry, is no less its concern than that of the professional ministers.

Recommendations

On the basis of assessments, feedback and other forms of dialogue, it makes recommendations to all agents of the congregation's ministry relative to elevating their effectiveness. This approach is always positive rather than negative and focuses on potential rather than problem.

Conflict management

It responds with immediacy to any conflicts, expressed attitudes, or real activities that might threaten or have an adverse effect on the congregation's ministry. The following postures govern the COM's actions of response to all such threats and adversities:

+ Actions focus on individuals and seek to avoid groups if possible.
+ Actions are motivated by redemption and seek reconciliation.
+ Actions are always attached to names (no exceptions).
+ Actions propose processes and refuse to permit the COM to become triangulated or to be forced into a position of providing the solution.

- Actions are always designed step-by-step and involve follow-up until the process is completed.
- Action processes reflect a refusal to allow issues to snow-ball.
- Actions are geared to what is best for the congregation's ministry and eschew private agenda or politicalization.

In brief, the COM only engages conflict and adversity management and refuses to be placed in a position of being responsible for conflict resolution.

None of the foregoing means that the COM is neutral. It is not because it must make judgments relative to effect on the congregation's ministry. However, it must assume a posture of maximum objectivity in order to make recommendations and establish redemptive processes. It seeks the resolution of issues to be by those who are directly involved in their creation. In finality, its decisions must be a firm advocacy of what is in the best interest of the congregation's mission-ministry fulfillment.

It may also arrive at a consensus that the issue that has been presented to it cannot be resolved. In such an event, rather than making a pronouncement of this conclusion, it presents information that makes the conclusion obvious and asks what more it can do relative to processing the concern.

Policies

The COM has a policy for all its members to follow that governs every possible contingency of its work and concerns. It is always immediately prepared to deal with any concern, issue, conflict, complaint, or suggestion. Examples are policies about assessing, educating, responding to complaints or suggestions, dealing with conflict, avoiding triangulation, making recommendations, certification and ordination requests, etc. (see addendum).

Confidentiality

COM members make a covenant of confidentiality and mutual honesty in respect to all deliberations. It operates on a high level of trust with the entire congregation, professional ministers, and staff. Without such trust its work would be totally ineffective. Thus, actions and postures that promote trust are paramount to its function.

In order to avoid confusion it is important for the COM to make a clear distinction between secrecy and confidentiality and to advertise this distinction. Secrecy, in respect to COM function, is understood to be a deliberate attempt to conceal information for the purpose of giving value to motivations such as devious control or unwarranted power. On the other hand, confidentiality is an attempt to give value to motivations that attempt to keep avenues of communication open for those who would otherwise feel hesitant to share their concerns:

- to honor people's need for privacy
- to facilitate the well-being of all involved
- to give time for resolving misunderstandings and conflicts without increasing and inflaming the issues involved
- to avoid harmful misinformation and gossip
- to deny the possibility of conflict escalation though unnecessary involvement and talk

The purpose of confidentiality is to facilitate the most expeditious means of redemption, reconciliation, resolution, or problem management as is possible and to do so in a manner that is least harmful and most enhancing to the congregation's ministry.

Power

The COM has no authority except that of recommending. Therefore, its power is derived from its stature. If it is functioning effectively, it needs no other authority. Indeed, paradoxically, having no appointed power increases its power because it functions from a stature that avoids negative responses to established authority and solicits responses geared to approaches of mutual concern, pooled wisdom, and ministry well-being.

Membership

Its members are selected with a critical eye toward the stature necessary for it to function effectively. Thus, the following criteria play a critical role in selecting its membership:

- An overarching commitment to the congregation's mission above all other agenda.
- An ability to see past the part to account for the whole.
- Capacity to keep confidences.
- Personal integrity. The ability to be caring while being honest and straightforward.
- The ability to listen.
- A willingness to make the tough decision.
- Membership stature.
- A minimum of three years of evidenced committed membership as a Unitarian Universalist.

Since the COM knows best the kind of members it needs and is normally privy to information not available to the average congregant, the COM presents a prioritized list of recommendations to the Nominating Committee to replace members rotating off the committee or leaving for other reasons. The

Nominating Committee, understanding the critical role the COM plays in the life of the congregation, gives these recommendations its own priority attention and ultimately makes its recommendation for replacement to the congregation at its annual meeting. If it is necessary to go beyond the COM's recommended list the nominating committee always solicits the COM's endorsement of further suggested candidates.

It is understood that no effective COM can be composed of people who represent facets of the congregation's ministry and who, therefore, become advocates of the part over the whole. Effective members will always be advocates of the whole. Wholeness is the only perspective from which the part can be adequately assessed in terms of its function because the part exits for the sake of the whole.

Further, there is a clear understanding that anyone serving on the COM must relinquish all other major positions of leadership in congregational life, owing to the need for objectivity in perception, a non-divided advocacy, and an often demanding time commitment. For the COM to achieve and retain its necessary stature, this kind of total independence from all other agents of ministry must be instituted and maintained. Thus, any member of the COM, upon assuming any other role of major leadership in the congregation's life, is obligated to resign from the COM. Ideally, aside from short-term projects, a COM member will have no other position of leadership in the congregation's life. Experience has proven this to be necessary wisdom.

It is also important to keep in mind that the minister attends all COM meetings but is not a member and does not vote. The minister's presence is invaluable to the committee's deliberations because of the information about both individuals and the institution that the minister embodies. While the committee should freely draw on the minister's knowledge and insights, under no circumstance should the minister be asked to represent the committee, either as a messenger or spokesperson. The minister has her/his own sphere of ministry and this sphere is distinct from that of the COM. In essence, the minister is a consultant to the COM but plays a different role in congregational life. It is important and vital to effective COM function to maintain this clarity between roles.

Rotation

The COM need not be large in numerical composition. Six members are normally sufficient. Moreover, small groups are able to deal more effectively with sensitive issues and arrive at a state of consensus. Membership is for three years with a staggered rotation. This keeps intact the committee's historical memory and wisdom. There must be an intervening year before any member leaving the committee can have membership reinstated. This precludes the building of membership dynasties and spreads the responsibility and experience around the congregation's membership and broadens the educational experience of service on the COM.

Accountability

The COM is ultimately accountable to the congregation. However, it reports to the board of trustees in between congregational meetings. While such reports may not be monthly, they are periodic enough to keep the board informed and aware of the COM's functional presence. All such reports are designed to protect confidentiality while alerting the board to the manner in which the COM is caring for the congregation's ministry.

Where a congregation has instituted policy governance, there is sometimes confusion about where the COM fits within the established lines of authority and reporting. Several distinctions should be made. One is the difference between the function of the COM and the function of the board and executive. The board acts on behalf of the congregation in-between congregational meetings and has been imbued with the authority to fulfill this function. When the board has assumed policy governance as its mode of oversight, it needs an agent to care for its traditional administrative and management functions. The executive is its designated agent for this purpose. The COM has no governance, administrative, or organizational management functions. Its primary function is to educate about the congregation's mission and ministry and assess all of its agents relative to their effectiveness of fulfillment and care for whatever conflicts might decrease the fulfillment of this effectiveness.

As suggested, the COM reports directly to the board when such reports are appropriate. It also may make recommendations to the board relative to raising the quality of the board's ministry. For example, the fact that a board has supposedly implemented policy governance is no guarantee that such implementation has been adequately done or is effective in terms of enhancing the congregation's ministry. However, the COM has no direct relationship with the executive except as, with the board, it might make recommendations to it about increasing its ministry effectiveness. The executive is not the board and the COM is not an administrative group for which the executive designs limitation policies. That is, the COM has no defined authority that needs executive administration. That it has only the power of its stature and recommendations is its unique character.

Policy governance policies are normally concerned with boundaries that indicate limitation of authority and, thus, give permission for certain creativity and activity to happen within these boundaries. While the board and executive concerns will be about the need, legitimacy, and violation of authority boundaries, the COM will have as its primary concern the effectiveness of the creativity and action that occurs within these boundaries. It is important to distinguish between effective policies that describe limitations of authority and the creativity and action that actually happens within the context of those limitations. Assessing the effectiveness of policy limitation is not necessarily synonymous with assessing ministry effectiveness. The COM would only be concerned about policy boundaries if they, in some manner, inhibited the fulfillment of the congregation's mission and ministry. And such concern would be very unlikely if the board and the executive were following the critical guidelines of true policy governance. Moreover, governance is about lines and powers of authority and ultimate control. Ministry is about fulfilling the religious mission of the congregation. While governance may be vital in how it is done, it is not an end to itself and constitutes only one aspect of how the congregation processes its ministry and should, therefore, be evaluated as to its ministry fulfillment effectiveness. Thus, the respective roles of the board, executive, and COM are quite distinctive.

The policies of board concerns are ends policies. That is, they are designed to speak to the broadest manner in which the congregation addresses its whole mission. The policies of executive concerns are means policies. That is, they are designed to speak to how various agents of the congregation's ministry carry out their specific mandates within this larger whole. The design of these combined policies is to permit maximum freedom and creativity on the part of both the executive and the congregation's ministry agents. The only issue that the board might have about the executive is violation of these larger policies. The only issue the executive might have with the board is whether or not its larger policies are too inhibiting or too permissive in respect to addressing the means of ministry fulfillment. Again, the issues here are with the nature of the policy being considered and its effect on creativity and action. On the other hand, the COM is concerned with everything that is happening in terms of the whole and the relationships within the whole as regards ministry fulfillment of mission whether it be authority, policies, creativity, or action.

It should also be noted that the board doing policy governance is not equipped to be a conflict management agent. Indeed, it normally plays a hands-off role in such circumstances unless one of the larger policies of its responsibility is producing conflict. Even if it strongly disagrees with the actions some ministry group has taken, unless policy violation is the issue then it does not act. And the executive's primary concern is with administrative management and organization and is generally not any more equipped to deal with conflict than is the board. And it behaves in the same hands-off manner as the board when it comes to disagreement with actions of ministry agents unless such actions conflict with its own established policy boundaries. And there is no reason for it or the board to be managers of conflict since their respective functions are not thusly designed. On the other hand, the COM is concerned about conflict and troubles that affect the congregation's ministry in negative fashion. And, if it is doing its job, it has policies that govern how conflict and other troubles are handled and is able to address such with immediacy and effectiveness.

Like the COM, policy governance is being tweaked in so many directions as to not be policy governance at all. This speaks all the more to the need for a body that is concerned only with the ministry of the congregation as it seeks the fulfillment of its religious mission.

Meetings

Monthly meetings are held with additional meetings called by the chair or agreed upon by the committee. These meetings are held in member homes in order to guarantee confidentiality. This confidentiality is for both its own deliberations and for those persons who might, by invitation, be attending its meeting.

The COM members cannot respond to issues in trust and honesty between themselves except in an environment that is conducive to such expression. This means an environment closed to the public. Moreover, people who wish to discuss confidential information with the COM will rarely do so if such a meeting is made public by virtue of its venue being at the congregation's busy facilities. The COM will fail without confidential environments for both of these purposes.

However, uninformed members of the congregation and those who might have private agenda are likely to question why the COM has closed meetings. "Why is it doing things in secret?" will be the question some will ask. This is why it is critical for the COM to be up-front about the difference between confidentiality and secrecy and why its meetings are confidential except when otherwise advertised. And it will have plenty of open meetings as it pursues its mandate of receiving information and having events for purposes of evaluating the congregation's ministry or educating toward its mission. Moreover, its individual members are invitingly open to all members who wish discussion. It is at its own routine meetings where confidentiality must prevail.

Policies

As previously indicated, having a set of clear policies that govern every facet of its functions is critical to the COM's effectiveness. Following are examples of such policies aside from those functions listed in its mandate:

1. **Internal membership policy:** a policy that indicates how it will recommend member replacement criteria for its membership, expectations regarding member behavior and attendance, replacement of members who assume other major congregational responsibilities, vacancies, etc. The committee must determine what constitutes an attendance record that warrants retention of its members. Non-attendance significantly decreases the wisdom and creativity pool of its deliberations. Moreover, members who do not attend the congregation's general and regular functions on a consistent basis will not be able to accurately assess the moods and needs of the congregation.

   Some of this policy may also be a part of the public mandate of the COM. Examples are membership criteria and length of membership.

2. **Contact response:** all members of the COM should be ready to respond in the same way to any member who poses an issue, expresses a concern, or proposes a suggestion for change in any area of the congregation's ministry. For example, it is useful to have a policy that governs such responses which requires a name be attached to all issues (assumption of personal responsibility), which requests that the concerned individual state the issue in a manner that potentially yields a positive resolution (refusal of the COM to be triangulated or to be responsible for a resolution), which confirms that the COM member has accurately heard what has been

shared (repetition of what is being heard), and which affirms that a process response will be communicated to the concerned individual in a timely manner (indicates a mechanism of feedback).

3. **Process policy:** a policy indicating that the function of the COM in reference to raised issues is to recommend a process which will project toward satisfaction or some possible resolution and which imbibes of the spirit of redemption (that the COM is not responsible for resolving such issues, only defining and helping facilitate a process or pointing in the direction of appropriate information which serves the same purpose or making appropriate recommendations of action).

4. **Conflict management policy:** a policy outlining how the COM will deal with issues of internal conflict between individual members and groups of individuals within the congregation. The goal of the COM is to manage conflict as opposed to resolving it. Indeed, the greatest danger of the COM is to allow itself to be drawn into responsibility for resolution. This is the quickest way for the committee to be disempowered in congregational life. Thus, the three cardinal rules are:
    *   avoid triangulation
    *   avoid triangulation
    *   avoid triangulation

Triangulation, in this respect, is to fall prey to the temptation of providing the solution or becoming the mouthpiece of any party aside from itself. Triangulation moves the responsibility for solution from the shoulders of those involved in the conflict onto the shoulders of the COM. This is why the COM's constant approach is to ask those posing complaints to offer a solution and those offering negatives to translate them into positives. While people may not always be able to fulfill this request, they are given the opportunity, and this reduces any criticism of how the COM recommends the issue be handled or what the ultimate resolution might be.

This means that the COM is only responsible for assessing the circumstance of the issue and designing a process that offers the opportunity of resolution or redemption. There are inevitable beginning steps in most every such design process:

+ Suggesting that the individual seeking help take the first step by approaching the person or group with whom the conflict is engaged with resolution or redemption in mind.

+ If the individual feels intimidated by this step, then the next suggested step is to offer for a member of the COM to attend the individual in making this approach (not speaking for but being present with).

+ If the individual is unwilling to take either of these steps, then the COM must either devise a different process of appropriate approach or ask the individual to cease pursuing the issue. It will be unlikely that there is another appropriate approach if the individual is unwilling to become responsible for helping process toward their own reconciliation. Thus, more often than not, the COM will be forced to take the hard stand of calling for cessation for the sake of the congregation's ministry. If the individual is unwilling to engage any steps suggested by the COM (including cessation of pursuit), then the COM may wish to go to the board with a specific recommendation as to how the board should act in the matter on behalf of the well-being of the congregation's ministry (and such may well be to terminate membership).

+ If the individual complies with steps one or two and the other party involved is unwilling to engage reconciliation, then the COM must, depending on the nature of the conflict, determine what steps to take to protect the ministry of the congregation, keeping in mind that the well-being of its ministry is the first priority. At this point, there are no formulas and creativity becomes the COM's primary activity. However, the COM, with no designated authority, will keep in mind that the board does have the authority to act on behalf of the congregation.

+ Hopefully, the process will yield reconciliation or some form of useful resolution so that the COM will not be required to invest further energy in the issue. If this is not the case, the COM must pursue the issue, in terms of process, until it finds some result that maximally favors the congregation's ministry well-being. And again, what this may be depends on the nature of the issue. Thus, COM insight, creativity, and determination become the focus of action. It should be kept in mind that this is not a form of triangulation, rather an activity protecting the congregation's ministry from harm.

Most of the COM's work will be free of that kind of stress that requires the individual member to clarify and prioritize personal values. However, entering into conflict management may well cause this kind of stress. That is, it may cause the members to assess whether friendship, or inclusion, or tolerance, or some other value is a higher one to them than the congregation's actual ministry. This is why it is so imperative to choose those members to be on the COM who have a proven record of holding the congregation's ministry up as their highest value.

The other thing to keep in mind about conflict management has to do with the committee's own perspectives. Whatever the issue under consideration, the COM should gain as full a picture as possible as to what lies behind the issue. During its deliberations, the COM may come to its own conclusions about the rightness or wrongness of the issue under consideration. This is natural. However, its function is not to process its own conclusions; rather, it is to establish processes that are designed to lead to redemptive results for those who seek its assistance. To insert its conclusions is to fall victim to triangulation. On the other hand, its conclusions may affect the design of the processes it creates, which is different from processing its conclusions. Or these conclusions may effect its recommendations to the board, if such need to be made. This may seem subtle, but it is substantive and is a critical distinction for the COM to maintain in its deliberations. Again, the COM may be forced to make a hard decision about cessation of conflict if no resolution is forthcoming, and it may even be required to recommend termination of membership if that appears to be the most likely means of protecting the congregation's ministry from harm.

Making the hard decision will always remain a difficult thing to do, despite the COM's devotion to the congregation's ministry above all else. However, with time and experience, the ability to avoid triangulation and develop the necessary processes that deal effectively with conflict will come easier.

While the COM resists the temptation to become the champion of its conclusions, nothing prohibits it from presenting the materials that has led to its conclusions as part of the management process. In this case, the materials speak the conclusions rather than the COM. Again, while the distinction between announcing its conclusions and allowing presented information to announce a conclusion may seem subtle, it is a distinction that empowers the committee with an objectivity that avoids triangulation while affirming the fairness of its efforts.

The bottom line is that the COM can set up an initial policy, such as outlined above, but only the actual experience of refusing triangulation and designing processes of reconciliation and redemption will enable the insight to broaden this policy.

5. **Follow-through policy:** a policy outlining how the COM will follow through in responding to individuals who bring issues or suggestions to its attention. This guarantees that any issue or suggestion brought before the COM will not only be addressed but will be followed through in its processing until it finds either a resolution, an implementation, or achieves the limits of COM responsibility.

6. **Appeals policy outline:** a policy that moves an unresolved issue, at the behest of the individual, through an appropriate sequence of steps until the highest body of appeal is addressed. An example would be to begin

with the individual or group involved seeking resolution, move to the COM if such fails, address the board of trustees when nothing has been successful, and finally appeal to the total congregation at a called or regular meeting. Such a policy both channels concerns to the right body at the right moment and indicates that the member's ultimate body of appeal is the congregation, itself. This policy must be endorsed by the board since the COM has no authority except that of recommendation. Moreover, in my experience, this process has never moved past the COM because the individual/s involved know that the board will review the history of the issue, and if those involved have sincerely tried for redemptive resolution, it normally will have been accomplished.

7. **Education policy:** a policy designating all the ways the COM will not fail to educate the congregation in respect to the congregation's mission and ministry.

8. **Assessment policy:** a policy indicating the rhythm, calendaring, and means of assessments in respect to the effectiveness of professional ministerial leadership and the church's ministry as a whole.

9. **Recommendation policy:** a policy indicating how assessment results will be used and how ensuing recommendations will be stated and processed.

10. **Visibility policy:** a policy designating all the ways the COM will not fail to make itself visible in the life and ministry of the congregation. Such assumes that the effective function of the COM is dependent on maintain-

ing a high level of congregational visibility. Such visibility often involves special name tags, mission-covenant renewal services jointly led by the ministers and members of the COM at the beginning of each church year, a brochure explaining the purpose and functions of the COM, a newsletter column, a presence at new member orientations, reports to the board of trustees and to the congregation at its annual meetings, public forums that process assessments or engage educational issues, etc.

11. **Certification and ordination policy:** the COM will explore requests for certification to perform weddings and memorials on behalf of the congregation and requests to be ordained to the professional ministry by the congregation. The conclusion of such exploration will be a recommendation (either pro or con with reasons) to the board of trustees in respect to the request. Again, this policy needs the endorsement of the board of trustees since this is a function the COM is fulfilling on behalf of this body.

12. **Ministerial inclusion policy:** a policy ensuring that all meetings of the COM are open to all called and settled ministerial leadership (or to the agreed upon representative/s) and that the voice of this leadership will be sought and valued in committee deliberations. Further, in the event that issues are to be brought before the COM regarding the effectiveness of a minister's leadership by parties outside of the COM, the COM and the minister will deliberate the wisdom of the minister's presence at this meeting. If there is no decided opinion in respect to this deliberation, the minister will make the final decision.

Whatever the decision made in this respect, it will reflect on the level of trust that exists between the committee and the minister (this sense of inclusion should be a part of the by-laws that define the membership of the COM). If the level of trust is not high enough to permit the minister to allow the COM to meet without his/her presence, then two possible issues need to be addressed. Either the COM has not been well constituted or the minister has an easily threatened ego. In either case, the work of the COM will be sabotaged.

13. **Congregational membership termination and cessation of attendance policy:** a policy indicating the circumstances under which the COM will make a recommendation to the board of trustees in respect to the termination of an individual's membership or a recommendation suggesting that a person be asked to cease attendance at congregational activities.

The foregoing are indicators of the need for policies that keep COM responses and decision-making activities consistent and motivated by the group's accumulated wisdom and redemptive approach.

The value of having policies in place is that they are immediately available for application and their creation is not freighted with the potential emotional and conflictual content of the circumstance that calls forth their needed guidance.

Conclusion

The success of this model is largely due to three factors: the model itself, the makeup of the committee, and the support of the professional minister.

The Model: the model presented here makes no assumption of perfection. However, when applied as is, it has worked smoothly and effectively over a long span of congregational ministry. Smoothness and effectiveness of function have not precluded the making of difficult decisions nor guaranteed a stress-free environment. But such characterized function does imply a successful protection and enhancement of the congregation's ministry.

The Committee: in a time in our history when our essential religious mission has been lost to other concerns, it is not always easy to find a group of people who value the institution's well-being above the call of friendship and the lure of private agenda. One of the reasons this model has worked so well is that in its past application the nominating committee has given this committee's membership a priority above all positions of congregational leadership other than that of the congregation's president. I suggest that such prioritizing has effectively kept the COM's membership at its highest level and, thus, its work at its highest level.

The Minister: it cannot be overemphasized that the devotion of the professional minister to the COM's effective function is critical to its success. This means that the minister must not only be open to receiving friendly suggestions in respect to the improvement of his/her ministry effectiveness, there must be sufficient ego strength to assume this posture in good humor and without a sense of threat. COMs can fail as easily because of this lack of ministerial devotion and ego strength as they can because of inadequate policies and members who lack the will to place the well-being of the congregation above the private agenda of themselves or other members. In brief, the COM will likely fail, irrespective of the model used or the character of the committee, if it does not have the wholehearted support of ministers whose devotion is to the mission and ministry of the congregation above their own private agenda, vocational issues, or ego needs.

Question

The following question is sometimes asked as regards the difference between the Ministerial Relations Committee and the Committee On Ministry:

"If the minister meets with the COM and that body makes recommendations regarding the minister's compensation and deals with issues congregants may have with the minister, what keeps the COM from being liable to the same discount of 'living in the minister's back pocket' as is so often leveled at an MRC?"

Discounting: Discounting is a common human defense mechanism. It is often an emotional response to something with which one does not wish to agree or which poses a threat to one's sense of well-being. When it has a strong emotional base it may also lack evidential support. Because the COM inevitably deals with sensitive issues in congregational life it will always be subject to whimsical discounts. Here are a few things the COM can do that will help diminish the possibility of this discount:

- It can educate the congregation about the significant differences between the MRC and the COM.
- It can refuse to be set up for the discount by not allowing itself to be triangulated.
- It can carefully guard its reputation of seeking maximum objectivity.
- It can be sure that its membership is of a stature that makes such discounting to appear to be what it is, an insult to lay leadership.
- It can be careful that the minister never speaks or acts on the committee's behalf.

- ✦ It can posture itself as valuing the minister's wisdom but of making up its own mind and keeping its own counsel.
- ✦ It can educate the congregation as to its role of advising all of the agents of the congregation's ministry in terms of improving effectiveness, including the minister.

Function: While the function of the MRC is to promote good relations between congregants and the minister, the function of the COM is to promote the well-being of the congregation's total ministry. This difference of purpose is radical in terms of the scope of the function of these respective bodies. The MRC highlights its relationship to the minister while the COM highlights its relationship to the entire congregation.

Visibility: Because the MRC's sole purpose is to promote good relations between the minister and the congregation, that is always the issue of its visibility. On the other hand, the COM is interested in all issues affecting the congregation's ministry and will be visible around all such issues. This multiplicity of visibility shows the broader scope of the COM's concerns beyond those that might focus on the effectiveness of the minister.

Advocacy: When there is an issue about conflict between members and the minister, the MRC, in seeking the restoration of good relationships, easily falls into the trap of becoming the advocate of the minister. When the COM confronts such an issue, it deliberately avoids making public judgments. Instead, it seeks to involve all the concerned parties in a process designed to bring about a redemptive result to the issue. Thus, the COM is always an advocate for the success of the congregation's ministry, rather than an advocate for any particular leadership responsible for that success, whether that leadership be laity or professional minister. This may cause the COM to make recommendations to the professional minister as well as recommendations to members of the congregation or its agents as regards such issues of conflict. It is part of the educational responsibility of the COM to position itself in the manner of its advocacy before the congregation prior to the possibility of such potential conflict.

The charge of "living in the back pocket" of the professional minister is, in reality, an insult to the lay leadership of the COM. It suggests that within the context of conflict, laity that advocates for the congregation's ministry will always side with the professional minister instead of with the congregation's ministry, which is its mandate. An effective COM will learn how to deal with such insults in a manner that further elevates its stature of leadership.

The issues of function, visibility, and advocacy tend to bind the MRC and the minister together into an inseparable unity, while the opposite is true with the COM. With the COM, the relationship with the minister is that of a partnership of separate entities (lay leadership and professional leadership) in the promotion of that ministry which fulfills the congregation's mission. And, if the phrase "back pocket" refers to ownership, the effective COM and the effective minister both live in the back pocket of the congregation whose mission they serve. And if the congregation understands this, then such charges will become ineffective ways of discounting the work and role of the COM by those with private agenda.

If the COM is being effective, it may well garner such back-pocket discounts by those who are unable to manipulate a preconceived outcome when resorting to the COM's service. It must accept that liberals are humans who posture spiritually unhealthy behavior and attitudes, and that they may become the brunt of such ill health in the same way that professional ministers become the brunt of member ill health. The COM's ultimate function is to help preclude such ill health from negatively affecting the congregation's ministry, irrespective of its source.

Resources

Mann, Alice. *The In-Between Church: Navigating Size Transitions in Congregations.* Alban Institute.

Mann, Alice. *Raising the Roof: The Pastoral-to-Program Size Transition.* Alban Institute.

McIntosh, Gary L. *One Size Doesn't Fit All.* Fleming H. Revell.

Schaller, Lyle E. *Looking in the Mirror.* Abingdon Press.

Size Transitions in Congregations. ed. Beth Ann Gaede. Alban Institute.